ONE PILOT'S STORY

THE FABLED 91st
And Other
8th AIRFORCE
Memoirs

Andy Anderson

authorHOUSE™

1663 Liberty Drive, Suite 200
Bloomington, Indiana 47403
(800) 839-8640
www.AuthorHouse.com

AuthorHouse™
1663 Liberty Drive, Suite 200
Bloomington, IN 47403
www.authorhouse.com
Phone: 1-800-839-8640

AuthorHouse™ UK Ltd.
500 Avebury Boulevard
Central Milton Keynes, MK9 2BE
www.authorhouse.co.uk
Phone: 08001974150

© 2006 Andy Anderson. All rights reserved.

No part of this book may be reproduced, stored in a retrieval system, or transmitted by any means without the written permission of the author.

First published by AuthorHouse 4/11/2006

ISBN: 1-4208-9148-0 (sc)
ISBN: 1-4208-9147-2 (dj)

Printed in the United States of America
Bloomington, Indiana

This book is printed on acid-free paper.

AN AMERICAN STORY

Andy Anderson

JOHN McCAIN
UNITED STATES SENATOR
WASHINGTON, DC 20510

One Pilot's Story: The Fabled 91st and Other 8th Air Force Memoirs
Dr. Andy Anderson
Foreword by Senator John McCain

As our greatest generation slowly recedes, and their tales of heroism are relegated to the pages of history, learning their stories takes on greater significance. I thank Dr. Andrew Anderson for taking the time to put his story on paper, so that it might be shared with future generations who will not have the privilege of knowing him.

The greatest generation was united not only by a common purpose, but also by common values-- honor, courage, service, and, above all, responsibility. Their lives, and ours, were forever changed by their struggles.

Millions of Americans left everything they knew to fight against a cruel and formidable enemy bent on world domination. They fought not just for themselves and their families, but for love of an idea – that America stood for something greater than the sum of our individual interests.

Deep-seeded courage marched with the sons of a nation that believed profoundly in itself, in the justice of its cause, and in its magnificent destiny. Americans went into battle armed against despair with the common conviction that their country believed it was worth their sacrifice.

As the members of the 91st know all too well, many paid the ultimate sacrifice. But an America worth dying for is worth living for, and those who returned home brought back an even deeper love of country, evidenced by the author's reflections.

Dr. Anderson's informal tone denotes the honesty and reality of his story. He gifts his readers a familiarity they might expect from a parent or grandparent, recalling their days off the coast of Japan, or in the fields of Germany. History buffs will delight in the detail, and future generations will be grateful for another precious account from our greatest generation. To Dr. Anderson, who reminds us freedom is a blessing that must be defended, thank you.

John McCain
John McCain
United States Senator

91st Bomb Group (H)
Madame Shoo Shoo
322nd Squadron

♪ Serenade in Blue-

Serial # 337707 LG M
Back Row – Left to Right:
S/Sgt. H. T Malon, Engineer (New Jersey); S/Sgt. S. B Blakely, Radio Operator (Arkansas); S/Sgt. C. P. King, Armorer Gunner (Idaho); S/Sgt. E. N. Waller, Top Turret Gunner (Mississippi); S/Sgt. B. J. Katewski, Tail Gunner (Iowa); S/Sgt. A. W. Shockley, Ball Turret Gunner (Oklahoma).

Front Row – Left to Right:
1st Lt. Thomas Gordon, Pilot (Lakewood, Ohio); 1st Lt. Andrew "Andy" Anderson, Co-Pilot (Los Angeles, California); 1st Lt. Jack Swisher, Navigator (East Liverpool, Ohio); 1st Lt. Mitch Maged – Brooklyn, New York

To: aanderson@socal.rr.com
From: Frank Farr
Sent: Sunday, August 29, 2004   6:49 PM
Subject: Combat losses

    Hi, Andy. I read your "39 of 36" piece. I calculated once that while we were flying 36 ship groups, we lost 41 in a three month period. This was an unscientific count while I was still flying, but the point is the same. Early on I calculated that my chances of ever finishing 35 missions were virtually nil. I thought I had a good chance, though, of becoming a POW instead of a KIA. That's the way it happened. I agree that everybody who ever climbed into a B-17 for a second mission over Germany was, in a way, a hero. We headed for combat missions knowing that we were certain to be shot at, and that we were fairly certain to lose anywhere from 9 or 10 men to as many as 100+ every time we flew. I remember my very first day in the 322nd, when I was looking around for a bed, and one young officer said, when I threw my bags on a certain bunk, "I wouldn't pick that one. Two guys who picked it in the last couple of weeks are gone." One can't really blame those who opted out, but we can be proud we weren't among them….. How's the book coming? I want to buy one when it becomes available.---- Frank F.

    From Andy to Frank: Believe me, Frank, you won't have to buy one.

Wee Willie going down
Only two more planes lost
1-Peacemaker - April 12th, 1945
2-Skunkface – Ap ril 17th, 1945 n*one lost on last mission*=Pilsen – April 25, 1945

They flew home.
Navigator and Bombardier killed in plane in top photo

xiv

PILOT

Pilot's Instrument View (Instrument View/F4)

1. Voltmeter (AC)
2. Radio Compass
3. Flux Gate Compass
4. Hydraulic Oil Pressure Gauge
5. Pilot's Directional Indicator
6. Pilot's Localizer Indicator
7. Altimeter
8. (x4) Propeller Feathering Switches 1 = Engine One, etc.
9. Airspeed Indicator
10. Directional Gyro
11. Rate of Climb Indicator
12. Flight Indicator
13. Turn and Bank Indicator
14. (x2) Manifold Pressure Gauges
15. (x2) Tachometer (RPM)
16. Landing Gear Warning Light
17. Bombes Call Light
18. Tail Wheel Lock Light
19. Flap Position Indicator (Up/Down)

Pilot's Control Panel – Left

20. Ammeters
21. Generator Switches
22. Battery Switches
23. Hydraulic Pump Servicing Switch
24. Voltmeter Selector
25. Inverter Switch

Pilot's Control Panel – Pedestal

26. (x4) Ignition Switches (Magnetos)
27. (x4) Fuel Boost Pump Switches
28. (x4) Fuel Shut Off Valve Switches
29. (x4) Cowl Flap Control Valves
30. Landing Gear Switch
31. Wing Flap Switch
32. (x4) Turbo Supercharger Controls
33. Turbo and Mixture Control Lock
34. Throttle Control Lock
35. Propeller Control Lock
36. (x4) Propeller Pitch Controls
37. (2x2) Throttle Controls
38. (x4) Mixture Controls (Lean-Rich)
39. Recognition Lights/Running Light Switches
40. (x2) Landing Lights Switches

CO-PILOT

Co-Pilot's Control Panel – Right

41. (x4) Intercooler Controls

Co-Pilot's Instrument View

42. (x2) Cylinder Head Temperatures Gauges
43. (x2) Fuel Pressure Gauges
44. (x2) Oil Pressure Gauges
45. (x2) Oil Temperatures Gauges
46. (x2) Carburetor Air Temperatures Gauges (behind column)
47. Free Air Temperature Gauges
48. Fuel Quantity Gauge (US Gallons)
49. Carburetor Air Filter Switch
50. (x4) Oil Dilution Switches
51. Engine Starting Switches
52. Parking Brake Control
53. Engine Fire Extinguisher Controls

An American Story

There were not many of us left alive. The maelstrom of battle in the air took an unbelievable toll of those heroic young men who volunteered to man the flying machines whose mission was to so damage the resources and materiel of the Third Reich that a large scale invasion of occupied Europe could be launched and carried to a successful conclusion. We completed that mission but a large part of the best of young America died doing it. They were the 8th Air Force, and they were all volunteers. This will be their story, but that story has been told, in part, in many places and many ways, so this will also be my story, from a point of view and experience that is both that of my comrades of those days, and mine alone.

Let me tell you some of the history and share with you some of the lives of those aircrews and airplanes which arrived in Britain as soon as possible after Pearl Harbor to begin the long process of wearing down the Nazi war machine, so that an eventual successful invasion of Hitler's "European Fortress" could be launched. Several detailed histories and several personal accounts have been written of what happened to prepare the way for the massive invasion and follow-up battles necessary to destroy the 'evil axis' which conquered and enslaved much of the western world and Asia. Those stories, written as 'history' have been well told in Roger Freeman's book, "The Mighty Eighth" and similar books, and other, more personal stories of those perilous times have been written, but I think the world is not aware of the unparalleled bravery and skill of those thousands of young airmen, all volunteers, who dedicated, and in many cases gave their lives to make possible the completion of that enormous task into which we were pushed by the heinous treachery of Pearl Harbor. Those men, in many cases were, or would have been, your grandfathers.

Early on, in the progress of the conflict in Europe, when everything looked grim for the then-allies, president Roosevelt asked for an estimate of the "over-all production requirement" to defeat our "potential enemies." Senior veterans Harold George and Ken Walker, with Larry Kuter and H.S. Hansell, were members of the group which was asked to make this judgment. They predicted that we would need, in order to defeat our then and potential enemies:

> 2,200,000 men
> 63,400 airplanes, in
> 239 combat groups, together with 108 separate squadrons not formed into groups.

As of 1945, we actually ended up with:

> 2,400,000 men
> 80,000 airplanes, in
> 243 combat groups.

The organization and production effort that went into the above, plus the simultaneous production and organization of the necessary accompanying war effort, is simply mind-boggling, but with Roosevelt's inspired direction and leadership, we did it, and we did it so well, that only five months after Pearl Harbor, in April, 1942, just before I graduated from high school, the 91st Heavy Bombardment Group was activated at Baton Rouge, Louisiana. There was little time for training. The Allies in Europe were in a disaster mode, so on September 25, 1942, the first wave of 91st B-17s left Bangor, Maine, for England. They were not the first to arrive. In June of 1942 a group of B-17s took off from Presque Isle, Maine, headed for England. Not one of them made it. Flight conditions were so difficult, and navigation skills so rudimentary that it was not until July 1st that the first B-17 arrived at its destination in Europe, Prestwick, Scotland. This airplane, B-17 E-41-9085, led a mighty armada of heavy bombers to England. In this first flight effort, five

B-17s and six P-38s were lost, although all crews were saved. The 97th Heavy Bombardment Group, the first Heavy Bombardment Group to arrive in England, settled in. It was soon followed, on June 25th, by the first of the 60th Group's C-47s, the transport workhorse of the 8th Air Force, and then by other Heavy Groups, including the 91st, which arrived at Kimbolton on October 1st. Colonel Stanley Wray, who had led the Group through its all too brief training period, and on its journey from Bangor to Kimbolton, could see that Kimbolton was not what he needed as a home base for the 91st, so he explored the English countryside. About 14 miles south of Cambridge and 100 miles north of London, next to a small town named Royston, he found an RAF training base with already built heavy concrete runways, capacious hangers, and steam heated barracks. Wimpole Hall, the Kipling family home, was within easy walking distance. It immediately became the commanding officer's residence, with the resident herd of cattle becoming the horned guard for the duration. On October 14th Wray simply moved the 91st in, informed the 8th Air Force headquarters, in London, that they were there, set up shop, and began training. Again the training was brief. On November 2nd they flew their first combat mission, to Brest, France, to hit the submarine pens which were housing the submarine fleet that was sinking so much of the Allied shipping that there was beginning to be some doubt as to whether the Allied merchant fleets would ever be able to deliver enough war materiel to England so that an invasion of the continent and subsequent defeat of the Axis forces would ever be possible.

The 8th, in its initial bombing missions, was feeling its way. It was imperative that something be done to lessen the disastrous effect which the German submarine fleet was having on the Allied supply effort, so at least eight of the 91st's first 13 completed missions were flown against the German submarine installations on the French coast. The other five were flown against airfields and locomotive shops near the French coast.

I note that 13th mission, flown against the U-boat pens at St. Nazaire, because that was the ninth mission flown by the Don Bader crew, during which he and the bombardier, Jim Hensley, were both so badly wounded that it was many weeks before either of them could fly again. As a matter of fact, Lt. Hensley was never assigned to fly combat again. When he returned to limited duty he spent some weeks as the assistant operations officer of the 322nd squadron of the 91st. Then, on May 3rd, he was ordered back to the "Zone of the Interior", (the United States) to complete his recovery. His injuries were so severe that they shortened his life. He was the father of Cindy McCain, the wife of one of our greatest national heroes, who spent five torturous years in a Vietnamese prison, Senator John McCain.

Don Bader, the pilot of that crew, eventually returned to flight status and resumed his missions. He was one of the very few early fliers from the 91st, or any other of the heavy bomber groups, who completed his missions and returned home to the States. He was later killed in a flight accident, there. Somewhere between three and five percent of the crews who flew those early missions survived.

I have a special interest in that crew, because before long, now, I intend to tell you of my own history in that legendary 91st Heavy Bombardment Group, but there are other stories which I must share with you, first. The story of the Bader crew is one of them, and my knowledge of it came about in this way:

About a year ago a 91st buff, who is also a computer buff, established a computer site for the 91st Bomb Group. About that time an Air Memorial Museum in Palm Springs decided to hold a memorial program for one of the more famed of the combat groups in World War II. They chose the 91st. As I said in the first line of this writing, there are not many of us alive, but they found about a dozen of us in Southern California, and invited us to share some of our war memories with their audience. Several of us accepted and afterwards had dinner together at our hotel in Palm Springs. I was fortunate enough to be seated next to Bert Humphries. We shared experiences and memories. Bert's were so fascinating that I asked him to share them with me in a computer message. One of the things we discussed at dinner was the battle losses of the 91st during the time that we flew. Bert said he had a list of the planes and crews lost during the time that the Bader crew flew (he was the copilot on that crew until battle injuries incapacitated him, after which he became the operations officer for the 322 squadron—later my squadron).

He said he would share that list with me. I had already researched the losses of the Group during the time that I flew, and I wanted to compare the Group losses during those two time periods. I found the loss rate decreased very little. The average number of missions completed during the early months of the 91st's combat time was five. Then the plane (and crew) was shot down. The average number flown when I flew was fifteen. Then they went down, or died. I went down on my fifteenth. The change in numbers was because there were few bombers flying when they began. There were hundreds by the time that I flew, but the loss rate remained close.

The normal assigned strength of a Heavy Combat Group was four squadrons of nine planes each, or thirty-six airplanes. By searching through the records that I could find of the time that I flew, from mid-June to September 5th of 1944, when I was shot down, I discovered that the 91st had lost 32 B-17s in that time span. Thirty two out of thirty six. That's a pretty heavy loss percentage. While the Bader crew flew they lost 38 out of their 36. More than 100%. Pretty rough. The Bader crew, on which Bert was co-pilot, flew on the very first bombing missions flown by the 8th Air Force. Bert said he'd go home, look up the record—(he'd kept careful records)—and share it with me. He did, and I'll share it with you.

Six of their first nine missions were flown in an effort to slow down the disastrous German submarine interdiction of the Allied supply lines. The submarines were destroying the Allied shipping at such a rate that it began to appear that an Allied army and its supporting units in England could never be built to the strength necessary to attempt an invasion of Europe, defended, at that time, by the all-conquering German army, navy, and Wermacht. The British daylight bombing effort had entailed such heavy losses that they had abandoned daylight bombing and concentrated on bombing at night, where their accuracy was not high, but the aircraft loss rate was not so strong that their bombing force would soon be eliminated, as it had appeared would be the result of their daylight loss rate.

Now came the Americans, with their huge, heavily armed bombers and their fabled Norden bomb sight. An immediate effort to crush the German sub pens began. Six of the Bader crew's first nine missions were flown against sub pens on the French coast. The other three were to locomotive shops at Lille, and air bases at Romilly sur Seine. At first the German pilots were wary. Many of them were veterans of the Russian front, brought west to aid in the forthcoming invasion of England, but the Russians had had no aircraft with the firepower of the B-17s and B-24s. Both the Americans and the Germans were experimenting, looking and learning. The first American bombing sorties were done as individual flights, but the German attacks soon began to take their toll, and Americans learned to concentrate their firepower by putting their bombers in formations which would allow the firepower of several of the bombers to support each other against the German attacks. The 91st first used this formation flying pattern on their 13th mission, on January 3rd, 1943, against the sub pens at St. Nazaire. The German fighter attacks were so fierce, now, however, that the Bader crew, for which this was their ninth mission, barely made it home. The bombardier, Jim Hensley, was so badly wounded that he never flew again, and the pilot, Don Bader, also severely wounded, was incapacitated for several weeks. When he did return to flight status, he completed his missions, returned to the "Zone of the Interior" (United States) and was killed some time later in a flying accident. During the time it took him to complete his missions, as Bert Humphries, later the squadron operations officer, related to me, the 91st lost 38 planes. This from a strength of 36 planes to a Group, you can see why there were few faces that I knew when I returned to the 91st after having been shot down, escaping from Europe, and returning to Bassingbourn. The loss rate stayed high. Few lived to return to the "Zone of the Interior" from those long, fierce battling months of 1942 and 1943. The loss rate decreased a little in 1944, but not much. During the short months that I flew, from June through early September of 1944 we, the 91st, lost 32 of our 36 planes in direct combat. Several others were lost in training flights and accidents of one kind or another. One of the groups not far from us lost a large part of its plane strength when a loaded bomber's bombs blew up on the flight line before it could taxi out for take-off. This kind of loss was counted as accidental, and not included in the combat loss count, but the planes were destroyed, and the crews were as dead as they would have been in combat.

ONE PILOT'S STORY

The P-51 that escorted us back from Kiel on Sept. 3, 1944

Let me share with you what happened to me in 1944, and then I'll go back and tell you what Bert Humphries and others' history was as the air war, or rather the American part of it, began, in November of 1942.

The best way that I can convey to you the events of that time is to quote from an article I wrote for an Air Force magazine some years ago. I'll do that, then I'll come back to this set of memories. This is what I remembered, and wrote. The first paragraph is a very brief description of my 14th mission. And I never would have thought I could put a description of that 8 ½ hour mission, on much of which it appeared the flak would get us in the next minute, the German fighters ripped through and through us, our wingmen disappeared, (shot down), the bomb bay doors hung up so that the engineer very nearly fell through them while trying to hand-crank them down, the engine which powered the cockpit heat was shot out, and I very nearly had a finger shot off by the same piece of flak—and the miraculous appearance of a P-51 was all that saved us—I never would have thought I could cover that in a few paragraphs, but here it is as I first wrote it for an Air Force magazine some time ago:

The flak bursts were heavy as the silvery B-17s of the 91st Heavy Bombardment Group approached Ludwigshaven on the Rhine River in the Ruhr Valley that bright morning in September of 1944. It had been a hard fighting, action filled week. Two days before, on Sunday, the 91st had been one of eight groups that flew a long, rough eight hour mission to bomb docks and airfields near Keil. Our number three engine was shot out by flak over the target. The lead ship aborted before the target run began, and the PFF (radar guided bombing equipment) malfunctioned over the target, so we came back over the Kiel Isthmus blind, and dropped our bombs by instinct. I wrapped a rag around my bleeding finger (from the flak hit that knocked out our # 3 engine), we feathered # 3 and pushed the other three engines to keep up with the formation, but we couldn't do it, so we dropped behind, sent the wingmen we had on, and braced for the fighter onslaught. It didn't come. A P-51, from heaven, picked us up and escorted us out over the North Sea to where we could head for home unescorted. If the P-51 hadn't been there the German fighters would have blown our lone B-17 to bits. Bless him. Never did find out who it was.

The bombing run just before we lost our engine had been a bastard. The Group had climbed to 27,000 feet to bomb. B-17 controls are mushy at that altitude, and, to add a problem, the bomb bay doors jammed when we tried to open them. Engineer Malon got them cranked down by hand just before "bombs away," then he cranked them back up. He slipped on the catwalk and lost his flak helmet out of the open bomb bay doors, cursing it out of sight as he wound the heavy doors back into the gleaming belly of the B-17. The cockpit heater worked off the lost engine. When it was shot out it got COLD in the cockpit—minus 70 degrees at 25,000 feet. Long four hour flight home from Kiel. Feet damn near frozen by the time we let down over the English Channel. The ceiling over England was down to 3,000 feet. We broke through just in time to see and join the Group in its landing pattern over the base. Prop wash almost threw us, but we landed O.K. Got home before the high squadron, even on three engines. After de-briefing we ate enough at one meal to make up for the one we'd missed because of the late take-off—12:35 from a 9:15 Group meeting and briefing.

The mission before that, # 12-B, (13) had been through flak-gun loaded 'happy valley' (Rhine) to hit an oil plant at Essen. Hammer flew low group lead. We flew lead of # 4 flight in the low Group, 200 feet below and just to the right of Hammer. Up at 3:30 for a 4:00 a.m. briefing. Plane stations at 5:40, engine start at 6:10, taxi at 6:20, and take-off at 6:40. Assembly over base at 14,500 feet. Two B-17s, from another Group, collided and went down in flaming pieces in front of us at 14,000 feet, just before assembly. We were all issued amber colored goggles to wear during heavy flak or combat, to reduce the chance of eye damage from fire or close flak, but I never wore mine. The sky is such a brilliant blue at altitude that I preferred to see the blue as blue, not amber, even during the extreme tension that we often flew under. At that moment, however, I wished I had the goggles on. The explosion was so close it nearly blinded me.

We climbed all the way from the coast to the target to reach the bombing altitude of 29,000 feet, and lucky we did. Flak was Hell all the way in. Thick enough to walk on 5,000 feet below us during the bomb run. Tom flew the run while I sweated. Used 2400 rpm and 46 inches of manifold pressure all the way. White smoke, and for some reason, red flame of flak burst was right with us for the eighteen minutes of the bomb run. Extra long run, today. Don't know why—and I've never seen red in the flak bursts before, but it was there, today. A burst under the wing of a B-17 above and ahead of us threw her into a beautiful slow roll. She recovered. It's a good thing the flak had blown the formation loose. Ships down and engines feathered all around, but only one small hit on us. A piece of flak came through the side skin, bounced off my flak suit chest and landed in my lap. Cut my finger, but I didn't report it. If they'd tried to repair it I'd have missed the next mission. It'll heal.

Mission # 12 had been to Ostheim Airfield near Cologne. We flew # 3 on Hammer's low Group lead. He took us in the prop wash of the lead group on the bomb run and it broke the group all up. Flak was heavy and accurate. The prop wash saved us. The two wing men of the wing leader lost and feathered engines. Several men killed and wounded in 91st planes. We had a few hits. Nothing drastic. Lucky. Shockley (tail gunner) saw bombs hit the airfield and string toward the hangers, but, in his words, he was "Too damn scared to see more." Several groups hit by Jerry fighters, today, but none came close to us. Flew "Choo Choo Lady". Good ship. Seven hour mission, five on oxygen. Cold as Hell. Heat in cockpit keeps us flexible and a little bit leaks down into the nose, so the navigator and bombardier can work, but the rest of the crew freezes. Minus 70 degrees at 25,000 feet. Went in and out by way of Brussels. Saw a lot of flak Jerry put up for the Limeys, who are flying some daylight missions, now. Dozens of Limeys around us as we let down. Rough mission. Made up for the milk run at Metz the day before. The day before Metz German fighters got six of our high group going into Leipzig. Only one plane from the 324th squadron got home. Lucky it was the 322nd's day to be stood down or we'd be gone, too. Don't know how we've been so lucky. On what was to be our third mission, to Leipzig on July 20th, we were scratched (stood down) at the last moment. The Group lost eight planes that day. Just our plane was scratched. We never knew why. Then, on August 16th, the day after Ostheim, the 322nd was stood down. We could understand that. We'd had terrific damage at Ostheim, but the rest of the Group had been hit just as hard. But the 8th went back to Halle (really Leipzig again) on the 16th, with the other three squadrons of the 91st leading the way, as usual, and they lost six planes, the whole 324th squadron. Could have been us, but we weren't there that day. And six weeks after we were shot down in "My Baby", on a mission to Meresburg on November 2nd, the 91st lost thirteen planes, six from the 322nd, five from the 323rd, and two from the 401st. That was almost the whole 322nd squadron, so if we hadn't gone down in "My Baby" on September 5th, we would have almost surely have gone down on November 2nd. And after that November 2nd mission there were only two crews left flying, other than Tom's, in our squadron, the 322nd. The squadron was quickly refilled, but our friends were gone. I'm just as glad I wasn't there to be a part of it, but I get a wrench in my gut when I think of it. Three quarters of my friends in the Group lost on that Meresburg mission alone, on November 2nd. Tom and our crew were almost finished by then, although each mission was a new crapshoot. They finished and came home, then scattered and never reassembled as a flight crew, but the Group was hardly recognizable by that time, in their eyes or mine. By the time the Meresburg mission was finished, on November 2nd, they had lost seventeen more ships. I surely would have been among them. I don't know how Tom and the crew stayed alive. I said at the beginning of this account, "I'm the luckiest man in the world. I'm alive." Other than Tom and the other members of his and my crew, not one of my friends from those days survived.

    I was kept in London for several days for an intensive interrogation concerning what we knew of the German troop placements and disposition in the area of France where we had been, and the location of the various bridges and facilities that we had de-mined and eliminated, and some other projects that we had undertaken. After we were returned to London we went our separate ways. General Doolittle signed a 'battlefield' promotion for me and I exchanged my gold bars for a silver set. When I got to see Colonel Terry on the base, I asked to be returned to my crew, but he said, "No. The rules set by the Geneva Convention required that 'escapees' not return to combat status, so I was to be returned to the U.S." That didn't make me too unhappy. My old crew was well on its way to a happy arrangement with a new co-pilot. They'd have lost me anyway. I'd been checked out as a first pilot, and I'd have been given a new crew whether I wanted it or not. So I said, "Goodbye", rode a train to Glasgow and sat on a ship's bow looking for the ever present submarines for a week, while journeying back to the "Zone of the Interior", the U.S. But I've strayed enough. Back to my story.

The morning of Tuesday, September 5th, I woke up to the insistent voice of the 'wake-up' sergeant.

"Lieutenant, lieutenant, briefing at 4:30." It was dark, except for the sergeant's flashlight. I looked at my watch. It was 3:30 a.m.

"I'm not up today. We're stood down."

"Yeah, I know, lieutenant. That's been changed. Your crew's up, but they have a new co-pilot, today. You're tapped to ride with a new crew."

"What crew?"

"New guy. Kelley."

I groaned and rolled out of my bunk. The scrambled powdered eggs and cold bacon in the messhall conspired with the drizzly, damp English weather to instill what seemed to me to be a permanent chill into my California bred bones. Briefing began at 4:30 in the briefing hut. I met pilot Bob Kelley, navigator Alton Karoli and bombardier George Lancaster at the briefing. We were to bomb a truck assembly plant at Ludwigshaven on the Rhine River. Our load was 4500 lbs. of incendiary bombs. I took notes on assembly altitudes and radio and flare codes, stuffed an escape kit with maps, passport photos and French and German money into my coverall pocket, strapped on a '45 pistol, struggled into my sheepskin lined flying suit and boots, and climbed into the truck for the ride across the tarmac to our plane for the day—a well worn B-17 with the name "My Baby" inscribed beneath the cockpit window. She was patiently waiting to begin her next mission over occupied Europe. For me this was mission # 15. It was Bob Kelley's second mission—the first for his crew. By 5:00 we were at the ship. I met the engineer, who monitored the gauges, but whose principal duty in flight was to man the rotating, twin machine gunned turret above and behind the cockpit. The belly turret gunner, the two waist gunners, the radio operator and the tail gunner were already aboard. The remaining guns, the nose side gun and the nose gun, were operated by the navigator and the bombardier in their spare moments. I was happy to see that ship was a G model, the newest model on the base. On the G, the nose gun had been replaced with a twin gunned chin turret, which, with its two fifty caliber machine guns, made a frontal approach by German fighters much more difficult.

Kelly and I pre-flighted the ship. He had had his first taste of combat two days before, riding as co-pilot on the mission to Kiel, where my crew's ship had had the engine that powered the cockpit heat shot out and we (in the cockpit and nose) had been frost-bitten on the way home. The rest of the plane was always in the grip of cold so bitter that frost was a regular flight companion (minus 60 to 70 degrees). Kelley's ship made it home that day with only a few flak holes, no serious damage or wounded crewmen. Two German Buzz-bombs putt-putted over while we were completing our pre-flight inspection. They hit in an open pasture just past the base. Too close—but no damage.

We started engines at 5:00 and sat in the take-off line. We were the last off, today, tail-end Charlie, but as we reached assembly altitude, 8,000 feet, we pulled into number two position on Tom Gordon, my own crew, in the fourth element. Some planes went out too far. Assembly was raised three angels (3,000 ft.) to allow the wing formation to tighten up before we reached the continent with its umbrella of German fighter craft.

At 20,000 ft. the flak was heavy as we crossed into Europe. The Wing zigzagged across the continent with an occasional B-17 drifting out of formation as it was crippled by flak blasts. Two red-orange blossoms flowered in the Group ahead of us as flak bursts found their fuel tanks. German fighters nibbled at the edges of the Wing formation. Our fighter escorts had either not caught up with us or were occupied elsewhere.

With a "thump" a piece of steel from a flak burst beside us chewed into our number three engine. It began jetting oil. We feathered (turned the stopped propeller edge-on to the air to diminish the drag) number three. The number four prop began to run away (overspeed). We feathered number four and dropped away from the formation as it turned onto its bombing run. With two engines gone, we couldn't keep up with the Group and had to get out of the path of planes and bombs now overflying us. The squadron leader, Captain Thompson, radioed "Good luck" and called for fighter support for us on the way home. The American fighters never found us, but five or six ME 109 German fighters began making passes at us. (Thompson was shot down two weeks later, and disappeared on his way to Switzerland).

The top turret, ball turret, tail and side guns were all chattering. The ship shook as she was wracked by shells from the German fighters. More German fighters, Focke-Wulfs, joined in the hunt. Word came through the intercom from the waist gunner:

"Doyle's hit, lieutenant." Then, a moment later, "He's dead." A burst from a German fighter lanced into our left wing. Number two engine began to burn. Kelley and I looked at each other.

"Time to bail out" I said. "We'll be O.K., Bob. See you on the ground." He rang the 'bail-out' bell. I said, over the inter-com, "Let's go, guys, all out."

The waist gunner's voice came over the inter-com.
"What'll we do about Doyle?"
"Nothing we can do," I said. "Go."

In a moment that seemed an eternity, as the German fighters roared past us and their shells ripped through us, came, "All out back here, and I'm going", ---then silence.

Kelley and I reached behind our seats, pulled out our chest pack parachutes, snapped them on, and , in what seemed one continuous motion, rolled out of the bottom hatch, which the engineer had thrown open, then exited, and through which the bombardier and navigator had just preceeded us. I had never jumped from an airplane. The quiet was almost deafening. The roaring sound of the plane, with its racing engines, rivet-bursting machine guns, acrid smell of cordite and blood, and atmosphere of imminent disaster, was instantly gone, and was replaced with a soft sigh of air, as I floated downward. I remembered to count to ten, and the count seemed to stretch interminably as I drifted gently through the air. Clouds covered the earth below and stretched as far as I could see. With nothing with which to compare my height and speed of fall, it seemed as if I were gentle, gently floating to earth.

I reached "ten" and pulled the rip-cord. The parachute snapped loose in front of my face and bloomed above me. An awful "whump" almost pulled me apart. I looked up at the white canopy above and watched a row of black holes stitch across it as a German Fock-Wulf screamed by and made a slewing turn to try again. Just then the clouds engulfed me. Blessed clouds. I would never curse their damp chill again. The German fighter roared past, but he couldn't see me in the thick cloud, and he flew off.

I broke out of the clouds at about 2,000 feet, with just enough time before I hit to see that I was coming down in the center of a tiny meadow surrounded by woods, with alternating green fields and woods all around. There were pops like firecrackers in the woods all around. There were pops like firecrackers in the distance. More black holes blossomed in my parachute. I hit the ground with my knees bent in a forward roll, and lay still with the half collapsed chute tugging gently at me. It was quiet. I stood up, collapsed the chute, unsnapped it from my chest, and looked around. Out of nowhere, it seemed, a woman came running to me. She stopped in front of me, looked at the collapsed parachute, grabbed it, stuffed it together, dragged it to the edge of the woods a few feet away, hid it under a bush, and came running back.

"Aleman ? " she said. I looked at her, blankly. She pointed at me.

"Anglaise ?" she said. I shook my head.

"No. American."

Her face lit up. "American", she said, and then said it again, as if the sound were a good, fresh taste. "American." Her face bloomed with a smile, then the smile disappeared as she grabbed my arm, pulled, and said, urgently, "Aleman."

I was a country boy, one year out of high school, trained only to fly. When she saw that "Aleman" was meaningless to me, she pulled me again and made a motion that even I could see meant urgency. The Air Force had recently commissioned me a pilot, an officer, and a gentleman. I had my doubts about the latter two, but I did want to fly again, so I ran after her as she disappeared into the edge of the woods, and began to run along a winding path along and up the hill. I heard the running feet of the German patrol as they entered the other end of the meadow. Jeannie and I ran quietly along the path up the wooded hillside for about half a mile. I was beginning to gasp, but she was still running lightly as a deer when she guided me off the path and up the hill into the thick brush. Five yards into the brush she stopped, kneeled, and pulled aside what seemed to be a part of the hill. It was a willow and leaf trapdoor, so cleverly made that not even a rabbit would have been able to discern the opening into the hillside. We climbed straight down a narrow shaft lined with logs, into which were inserted iron rungs as handholds. Jeanne pulled the trapdoor into place over our heads and waited, quietly, as the German patrol ran past. Only then did I notice the two men behind us, where the vertical shaft turned horizontal and became a small room in the hillside. The two men were Russian soldiers, Paul and Tim-o-fey, who had been captured at Stalingrad and brought far across Europe to Metz to work as slave labor, there. During a British night bombing, nearly a year before, they escaped from Metz, somehow found their way cross country from Metz to Baslieuse, where we now were, and had been hidden by Jeanne, her husband Rolland, and a French farmer, Jean Ney, who constituted what there was of an underground (resistance) in that area. I learned their story later. They spoke no English and little French, and I, of course, spoke only English. Jeanne pointed to them and said "Russky, Paul et Tim-o-fey." She pointed to me and said "American." Paul and Tim-o-fey hugged me, kissed me on both cheeks and heaped up straw to sit on, on the cold floor, where we began to try to communicate. I wasn't too sure about the cheek kissing but did learn to enjoy it, especially when it was offered as we passed through the largely male-less villages, and even more male-less Paris, when we eventually reached it, sometime later.

For now, however, Jeanne listened, beneath the trap-door, to make sure the German patrol was out of sight and hearing, then lifted it and was gone swiftly and quickly as a woodland fawn to seek other survivors from our plane. During the day she and Rolland brought in our navigator, Alton Karoli, the bombardier, George Lancaster, and pilot Bob Kelley. Bob's mother had been born and raised in France, then met and married Bob's father and moved to America, so Bob had been raised in a bi-lingual household and spoke fluent French.

The four of us were all Jeanne and Rolland could find. Four others had been able to exit the plane, but they could not be located. Since they had exited the plane before the four of us, they were further back toward the German border, and we thought, had probably been captured. The ninth crew member, the tail gunner, had been killed at his station and never exited the plane.

In the evening the French farmer, Jean Ney, brought us a chocolate cake. We didn't realize what a sacrifice this was. There was no food in the village. The Germans had taken it all, and there were almost no men in the village. The men had been taken by the Germans to Germany, to be used as slave labor to produce war materiel for the German war machine---the German armed forces had drained Germany of German working men, and much of the labor, in factories and on farms, was being done by slave labor, by men like Paul and Tim-o-fey.

The chocolate cake, welcome as it was, was a little hard to chew. It was liberally reinforced with sawdust and the wood chips were an obstacle. We were grateful, however. It had been a long time since breakfast.

The small passageway in the cave where the Russians, Paul and Tim-o-fey, and now we Americans lived, opened into a larger room. The cave had been dug during World War I and Frenchmen had hidden there from German conscription during WW I. The men from the village had hidden there again in 1939 when the Germans invaded, but over the years most of them had been captured and sent to Germany as slave labor. Jean Ney was left to work his farm and produce food, and the Germans never caught Rolland. Now, in 1944, the Germans retreating from the fighting at the invasion front confiscated all of the food as they passed through. Where Jean found the material for the chocolate cake we could only guess.

The rushes on the floor were damp and cold. Rolland brought us civilian clothes for later escape use. He brought what food he could find, usually raw potatoes. Once he brought his five year old son, and so impressed upon him the need for secrecy that the boy would not tell his sister in the morning where he had been the night before.

Rolland brought us water, and dumped in raw beet sugar. They had no wine, and could not conceive of drinking pure, unprocessed water. We crept into the village at night and shared some of their precious bread, with a large sawdust content—the wood pieces were large enough to interfere with chewing. When the German camp in the meadow extended up the trail toward our cave we slept in an abandoned shed which had once housed animals. The straw was vermin infested. We unknowingly brought the little beasties back to the cave with us. They were not welcome guests. Paul and Tim-o-fey slipped out to ambush Germans. They had no guns, but they were very skillful with knives and the Germans passing through had no way of knowing where some of their men disappeared to. The Russians came back grim but satisfied.

Tim-o-fey and I were younger and perhaps more venturesome than our cavemates and we were growing quite hungry. On one of our night trips into the village we lay beside a low hedge while a German patrol passed on the other side. The last soldier stopped beside the hedge, laid down his machine pistol, unbuttoned his pants, urinated over the hedge onto my shrinking back, buttoned up, picked up his machine pistol and hurried on to join his patrol. Tim-o-fey wanted to knife him on the spot, but I restrained him, so we were able to find a little food and rejoin our comrades. Another night we hid under a trapdoor beneath a rag carpet in the central room of the Jacob's tiny home while the German patrol inspected. One of the homes in the village had an elementary crystal radio on which they occasionally picked up BBC broadcasts. They told us the invasion was proceeding, but the Americans were not yet to Paris. We grew hungrier. The beasties chewed harder. The retreating Germans were pulling their artillery back with horses. American fighter planes were decimating their motor transport. Horses grazed in the meadow at the foot of our hill. Then one night there were no horses. There was no sound of Germans but we knew there would be more. And we had to be exceedingly careful when in or near the village. The village priest had a German background, and the villagers, though generally Catholic, did not trust him.

We had had some injuries. Bob's hands were bloody and damaged, and Lancaster, the bombardier, had landed in a tree and injured one leg so severely that Rolland and the other man who brought him in (we never saw him again) had had to carry him. George had been a heavy smoker, and the combination of a painfully injured leg and lack of nicotine sometimes almost drove him up the wall. We occasionally had to muffle him when we were afraid the Germans from the meadow below were getting too near. We were fortunate that the other three of us were non-smokers. And that was unusual. Cigarettes for the soldiers, usually free, were available everywhere. The nasty narcotic of nicotine dulled the misery of military life, but the addiction it produced occasionally almost destroyed us, as was the case with our bombardier.

Bob did not regret his bloody hands. Occasionally we pilots wore seat pack parachutes, but they made movement difficult. We generally preferred to wear the parachute harness, but to carry the chute, itself, as a chest pack, then snap it onto our harness if and as it was needed. When we climbed in the plane through the forward hatch, that day, carrying our chest packs, we each reached up and placed our chute pack behind our seat, where there was a small open space. After we dropped out of our formation and as the fighter attacks began to grow heavier, it began to appear that we would not survive, but we were 'jinking' the ship to avoid the fighter shells and we needed both hands on the controls. When it became apparent that we would have to jump before the ship blew up, each of us reached down for his chute, but it was too difficult a reach to get the chute behind the seat, so each of us reached across the aisle, picked up the other's chute and snapped it onto the chest rings on our parachute harness. The parachutes weren't personalized. We picked up a different parachute each time we flew. This day we snapped them on and almost immediately dived out of the hatch. I counted, for what seemed a long, long time, and then pulled the ring. It opened with an awful 'whump', almost pulling me apart, but keeping me in good shape. Bob's, which was really my chute, didn't open when he pulled the ring. He later told me that he looked at the ring, loose in his hand, uttered a few well-chosen expletives, and began to tear at the heavy canvas chute cover with his hands. Tearing that canvas loose and off with his hands was not possible, but he did it. Humans can do incredible things under stress. He did. He tore the cover loose, pulled the top of the chute out and tossed it into the air. It opened and behaved well. He floated to the ground, but his hands were bloody and torn and it took some time for them to return to normal use.

After several days we decided that the risks to our French friends were too great, and we were beginning to suffer seriously from lack of food. Paul and Tim-o-fey, who had a bitter hatred of the Gernans and were both very skillful with knives, picked off enough of the retreating Germans, usually when they were serving as sentries at a night camp, so that it appeared to us that the Germans would put on a serious search to find out what was happening to their vanishing soldiers, soon, and since we were now dressed in civilian clothes, supplied by Rolland, it also appeared to us that if we were caught we would simply be shot out of hand, as many of the villagers had been, with little apparent reason. The area we were in, Alsace-Lorraine, just across the border from Germany, had been bandied back and forth between France and Germany for generations. From the time of Bismark on, one nation and then the other had ruled the area, so that one village would be French in its sympathies and the next would be German. We were lucky. The ancestral history of Baslieuse was primarily French, but there was enough German sympathy near so that Rolland let us know how careful we had to be. We decided that to survive we had to move, and since George could now, to some extent, use his injured leg, we reclaimed our American clothes, put them on, and prepared to strike out across France.

The escape map in my pocket showed that we were about ten miles from the German border, near the cities of Metz and Nancy. Two smaller towns nearby were Longwy and Longyon. We lay awake for one last itching, scratching night, said "Goodbye" to Paul and Tim-o-fey and started for the village. Halfway there we were met with the news that "The Americans have come." Running to the village, we saw a beautiful sight---four Americans in a jeep, with rifles. With yells of joy we hugged the soldiers, then hugged our village friends, especially Jeanne and Roland and climbed in the jeep to go join the American forces, which, we presumed, were just down the road.

The jeep took off like a scalded bronco, coming to a stop almost immediately in the next village, where the people, seeing the jeep and the American uniforms, lined the street, holding out glasses and trays of Calvados and other liquors. The soldiers partook enthusiastically, we cautiously, and me, with my Mormon abstemious background, not at all, so that very shortly I was the only sober one in the jeep. I was the more sobered by the information from the four soldiers that they had no idea where the American forces were, that several days before they had tired of their weeks long assignment of unloading supplies at the invasion port of Cherbourg, had picked up their rifles, climbed in a jeep and headed for where they thought the "front" was, to do what they had come to Europe for, fight the Germans, before it was all over, with them still unloading ammunition at the beachhead. They had driven through the "front" and never seen it. They were looking for Germans to fight and found us.

Dusk was drawing on. There were no men, at least none visible, in this or any other of the villages that we passed through—only women. What men there were, and older boys, kept out of sight. They knew the Germans were still in control, but we didn't, although we were being enlightened. The soldiers wandered away with the village girls. We crewmen shared some food with a village family, then my memory blanks out. I was exhausted to the point of unconsciousness. Later Bob Kelley told me he took me to a basement room in one of the houses, dropped me on a bed, and locked the door. He didn't know there were two doors to that room. I don't know what Bob did. He and Karoli both had wives at home, and as far as I know they both remained faithful to them while we were in France—and it wasn't easy. I woke up the next morning wishing I were back with Paul and Tim-o-fey, who were sober and knew where the Germans were.

When their hangovers became bearable the next morning we persuaded our soldier friends with the jeep that the better part of valor was to advance to the rear, locate some Allied help, and then return to the fighting. As we drove on we discovered that most of the bridges over the streams and ravines had been mined, but the controls had been left for troops which were yet to retreat to activate, so we spent a good deal of time de-mining the bridges which we crossed. How we did this is beyond me. None of us knew anything about demolition, but I can remember unwinding the wires from bundle after bundle of explosives as we stopped to check the bridges we crossed. And the miracle of roads without Germans continued.

The soldiers drove us for most of another day toward where we presumed the 'front' was, then they repented of their 'retreat,' said "goodbye" to us, turned around, and roared back to find some action. We knew we had been involved in a miracle, driving more than two days through country crawling with retreating German units without meeting any. We gave our soldier friends our name and Group number. We knew they would be court-martialed for desertion when they returned to their unit, and we wanted to do what we could for then, but we never heard from them. Most likely they encountered angry retreating German soldiers within minutes of leaving us, and were quickly killed. We moved on as best we could, and eventually walked into an advanced American body collection station. There we climbed on a truck with a load of American bodies and rode west. We left the truck near the outskirts of Paris, and walked into that Queen city. The Queen was jumping. The main German force had pulled out, but the Allies had not entered in force and the FFE (resistance fighters) were systematically eliminating the remaining Germans. We later found that Hitler had ordered the general in charge to destroy the city as he left, but, believing he would be back, he refused. He left, thinking that he would soon return, but it was not to happen. There was a fierce battle going on within the city. A small German group was holed up in the Notre Dame Cathedral and the FFE were attempting to get them out without destroying the Cathedral with artillery. How they accomplished it I don't know, but they did, because the Cathedral was left standing. The fighting was still going on as we left, so I have not yet been inside Notre Dame cathedral. I hope to go back some day.

We found a room in a little hotel, paid for it with the escape money in our kits and watched the action in Paris. Kelley's facility with French was invaluable. I sat with him in a street café evenings as he was pairing up the senior Allied officers (senior, to me, was major and up) who had found a way into Paris, with the welcoming Parisian mademoiselles. It was wonderful how much happiness a little translation could achieve. I still have that enormous key to room 604 of the Mondotel at 22 Avenue Opera, in lovely Paris. I'm a little ashamed. Some day I hope to return it. Bob's comfortable use of French produced rewards for us that money could not buy. I came home with enough bottles of Chanel # 5 so that I could dole them out for many months back in the states.

When I began this look at a portion of history that I know so well I intended to tell of a part of the war in the air as I and others I knew lived it. Somehow I've been sidetracked into my own story, so let me do a little more of that, and then I'll go back to what I know of the air war and the men who fought it, from their point of view, and mine.

When we were returned to England we were kept in London for some time for an intensive 'debriefing.' The invasion had been successful, but the war yet hung in the balance. If Hitler had left Rommel, that brilliant general and tactician, in charge, the Germans could well have contained the invasion and destroyed the Allied armies. Not likely, but possible. But Hitler was insane. He forced Rommel to kill himself, and by doing so, insured his own destruction. We had done a little bit of damage on the way out and we knew the country. Intelligence wanted to talk with us, and they did. Far beyond our worth, it seemed to me, but we were well treated. General Doolittle dictated a 'battlefield' promotion for me and I happily exchanged my second lieutenant's gold bars for the silver of a first, far ahead of the time I would have achieved them, otherwise.

As our intelligence debriefing was closing I asked that our friends in Baslieuse, the Jacobs and the Neys, be given some help and recognition. General Eisenhower himself sent them a letter of thanks. Nothing else was ever done. Some time later, when I pushed for more information, I was sent this report:

A-3 Confidential:

"Intelligence reports indicate that the Russians, Paul and Tim-o-fey, were exposed to the Allied government by the collaborator, Father Paul. The Russians were transported to the Berlin sector and returned to the Russian army. Father Paul could not be located. The Jacobs have been located and will be helped if necessary."

After the war I wrote to the Jacobs. They were very poor. No further "aid" was ever given. Jean Ney owned a farm. Rolland Jacob scratched out a living as a road laborer. They raised a family. We sent packages.

After the mission to Ludwigshaven, when our plane disappeared with a swarm of German fighters attacking it and we were not heard from, the War Department sent a "Missing in action, presumed dead" telegram to my parents. The telegram was delivered to my father.

```
                                                              25/2
                       R E S T R I C T E D


                       HEADQUARTERS EIGHTH AIR FORCE
                         Office of the Commanding General

   SPECIAL ORDERS)
   NUMBER....265 )                       29 September 1944

                            E X T R A C T
        *                        *                        *

       5. The following O, AC, are DP, temp promoted to the gr indicated in AUS
   w/rank fr date of this order. (Auth:  Cir 90, Hq European T of Opns USA, 17 August
   1944):
                            1ST BOMBARDMENT DIVISION
        *                        *                        *
                            2nd Lt to 1st Lt
        *                        *                        *

   ANDREW W. ANDERSON JR, 0820930

        *                        *                        *

              By command of Lieutenant General DOOLITTLE:


                                              JOHN S. ALLARD,
                                              Brigadier General, USA
                                              Chief of Staff.

   OFFICIAL:
              s/ Lindsey L. Braxton,
              t/ LINDSEY L. BRAXTON,
              Lt Col, AGD,
              Adjutant General.

                                     A TRUE EXTRACT COPY:

                                        JOHN R. PARSONS, JR.
                                        Captain, Air Corps,
```

Man of magnificent faith---later, when I said, "Why didn't you show the telegram to Mother?" he said, "It was in God's hands, not mine." Mother later said that now she knew why the tears rolled down his cheeks when my phone call came from England that I was OK.

When my parents retired from a lifetime of teaching they traveled to Europe and visited the Jacobs. There is no train to the tiny village of Baslieuse, but they took a train from Paris as far as they could go and then they hired a taxi to take them the rest of the way to the village. The driver was reluctant to wait, so they bought him a bottle of wine and told him to drink it at his leisure. I don't know how they conveyed this, but he took an hour or two at his bottle, then came in and informed them that he was ready to leave. My parents left, reluctantly. They sent packages the rest of their lives. Later, my son, traveling in Europe for his computer company, searched for and found the Jacobs in their tiny house at the end of the house row in Baslieuse. When he came home, he was thoughtful.

"Dad, none of the people they saved have ever been back to visit them. You're the one they'd really like to see."

My conscience lurched. I was the principal of a junior high school in Northridge, a suburb of Los Angeles. My wife has taught, occasionally, but she has spent most of her life as a full time mother and homemaker. We have put three children through college then through professional school. The last one, a nurse, graduated in January, studied for her California license, and went to work last month. There has been little time or money for travel.

"Perhaps in five years, when I retire, son."

"Dad. It's been more than forty years. Jacob is seventy-six. Jeanne is in her late sixties."

At Christmas, Kevin handed me a small packet, but there was a twinkle in his eye.

"I'm sorry it's so small, Dad. It's been a tough year."

I said, "It's the thought that's important, son,"

I opened the package. Inside were two airline tickets to Luxembourg, the nearest airport to Baslieuse.. It was the first time my family had seen me totally unable to speak.

Kevin said, "If you'll go in April, I'll go with you."

We planned to go at school vacation time in April. I wrote the French Consul-General in Los Angeles, Monsieur Jean-Claude Moreau, to ask help in creating an award ceremony for the two families who had risked so much for us. He wrote back with Gallic enthusiasm and warmth. He made arrangements so that when we should reach Europe, in mid-April, we would contact the 'Director du Cabinet' in Meuthe et Moselle, the province which included Nancy, Longwy, and the tiny village of Baslieuse.

I wrote the Jacobs that we were coming. In early April Kevin, Virginia, and I flew to the Europe I had last seen more than forty years before. We stopped to see the shimmering mass of bloom that is Keukenhof, a national tulip garden of Holland, we glided on a steamer up the Rhine, through the watchful, medieval castled valley of the Ruhr, above which I had flirted with death so many times, and drove from Luxembourg to Baslieuse, which I had left so hastily many years before.

Because it is so tiny, in spite of the fact that Kevin had been there the year before, we drove right through the village before we knew it was there. After a consultation with a passing driver, who spoke no English, as we spoke no French, we drove back to the village center, where a group of people were waiting outside a small building.

I climbed out of the car and straight into the arms of Jeanne. Her lovely elfin face had a few more lines than it had four decades before, and she had added a few more pounds, but it was the same merry smile and loving person who had shared with us the food her children needed, and who had held me down behind the bushes while the German patrol ran by, machine pistols at the ready, more than forty years before.

Rolland had greyed a few more hairs and added a few lines over the years, but I got the same kiss on both cheeks from the same rough, wise face that had grinned at me when he climbed through the trap-door and brought in the other fliers so long ago.

The village mayor, Marcel Humbert, with his badge of office, a splendid red, white and blue tricolored sash wrapped around his waist, ushered us into the city hall, where all of the inhabitants of the village were gathered. I spotted the farmer, Jean Ney, and his wife, and was able to give them a hug before the champagne glasses on the table were lifted and the speeches began. The senator from the province of Meuthe et Moselle, Hubert Martin, was an orator with a lion-like mane of snow white hair and a deep, reverberating voice.

He orated. Antoine Porcu, the local deputy, (congressman) spoke. M. Maigret, from l'office de'partmental des anciens combatants (the office of veterans' affairs) spoke. The local military commander and the local police commander spoke, the Abbe Djemange, the village priest, blessed us, and all of this was translated for us by an ex French Air Force pilot, Bernard Wesoloski, now the curator of a local museum, who had come by to see what all of the excitement was about in Baslieuse. The interpreter promised by the 'director du cabinet' never appeared, so Bernard, who spoke excellent English, became our interpreter for the day. He was kept busy as the speeches, toasts, and awards rolled on. I had brought an illuminated scroll from the city of Los Angeles, signed by our mayor, Tom Bradley, an old friend, an award scroll from our Los Angeles Board of Education, and some personal gifts for the Jacobs and the Neys, but our friends, and the village, itself, with the warmth and affection so characteristic of the French, overwhelmed us with gifts. The municipality presented us with a magnificent renaissance style crafted plate, and I was presented with some personal medals, from the government and the municipality. Jean Ney had located our crashed aircraft, extracted a piece of metal from a cylinder wall, embedded it in a handsome wood plaque, and carved the Cross of Lorraine on one side, the Stars of the United States on the other, and a message of affectionate commemoration across the bottom:

Que ce fragment do bombardier dans lequel se trouvait Monsieur Anderson lorgqu il fut alattu en Septembre, 1944, relie nos deux nations et nos deux peoples comme it relie sur cet isusson.

Les etoiles des Etats Unis d'Amerique et notre croix du Lorraine Que Dieu nous garde de la Guerre.

(May this fragment of a bomber, in which Mr. Anderson was when he was hit in September, 1944, tie together our two nations and our two peoples, as it ties, on this board, the stars of the USA and the Cross of Lorraine. May God keep us from war.)

After the ceremonies the whole group trooped down the street to the village inn for lunch/dinner. It was a remarkable repast. Later, in trying to recall the meal, we could remember ten separate courses, with appropriate wines. There may have been more. We ate and talked away the afternoon, with Bernard doing a running, two-way interpretation. During the course of the meal, the deputy, Monsieur Porcu, moved around the room exchanging pleasantries with each person. A villager down the table leaned over to me, motioned to Monsieur Porcu, and, with Bernard's help, said, "You have politicians in America, too?"

We had begun toasts, speeches, and awards at 11:30. We went in to lunch/dinner at 1:00. We finished eating and talking about 5:00, then we all set out to visit the cave where we had been hidden. As we walked across the green fields and down the wooded paths where we had moved so stealthily years before, memories flooded back. We stopped at the cave where we had sheltered. It was broken open, but still recognizable. Then we moved down the path to the meadow where Jeanne had met me and hidden my parachute. She told me, now, that she had gone back there after we left, salvaged the parachute, and used it to make underclothes for her children. That parachute had served me well, but it had been Bob Kelley's. We remembered Bob's stressed fingers after he had done the impossible—he had torn through the canvas, thrown out the chute. It had caught, and he survived.

The meadow was tinier than I had remembered. We stood in the middle of it, where I had landed, and I remembered Jeanne's "Aleman, Aleman?" and her tugging at me to run as the German patrol rounded the edge of the meadow---and we disappeared up the hillside path on our way to the cave.

I remembered Bob's bloody fingers as Rolland brought him into the cave. We talked of what happened in the field, in the cave, and in the village. I shuddered as I remembered the risks Tim-o-fey and I had taken. One noise, one slip and the Jacob and the Ney families would have been executed. They knew it and we knew it---and they never hesitated. And now all I could do, in exchange for our lives, was to bring them an illuminated scroll signed by our mayor, a pair of sweaters, and a long, warm embrace.

We walked back across the fields to the village, to the Jacob's tiny home. As many villagers as possible crowded in. Rolland pulled aside the rag rug, opened the trapdoor, disappeared into the tiny root cellar that I remembered so well and came up with a bottle of clear, homemade cherry liquor. One sip set off a fire in my throat and an explosion in my head. We moved on to Jean Ney's home. More toasts. He slipped a bottle of the home-made cherry liquor into my pocket. I brought it home with me. Liquid dynamite. The level has gone down an inch in the intervening years.

At the lunch/dinner an old farmer leaned over and said to me, through Bernard, "We hoped to see you, again. DeGaulle did not want us to be such good friends with Americans, but we know what you did for us. We would like always to be friends."

Dear brave, kind, warm, generous French friends. I look at the picture we took, in the meadow, of our son standing between the two Jacob sons. My son is there because the Jacobs and the Neys risked their lives and their children's lives for us so many times. We love them.

We returned."

That account was published as a part of the publication, "Memoirs of the 91st Bomb Group," by the Turner Publishing Company.

A flier friend of those days sent me a message over the Internet. He said,

"Andy, I just read your piece in the 91st Group "Memoirs"—a great story well written. I was particularly interested in your account of Kelley's rip-cord failure. Exactly the same thing happened to me at Meresburg. I fell free until I reached what I thought to be about 10,000 feet, in order to escape the intense cold and marauding FW 190s up where we were—about 25,000 feet. Then I pulled the rip-cord and NOTHING. I looked at the red handle, threw it away and began clawing at the front of my chute, just as you say Kelley did. It worked or I wouldn't be telling you my story. I wonder how many luckless airmen died because it didn't occur to them to try to get into the chute after the ripcord failed to work, or because they were too paralyzed with fear to make any further effort.….It's wonderful that you were able to go back and see your French friends later. I'm recovering from surgery, probably a belated effect of the months I spent in a German prison camp. Yes, they were barbarous. I'm glad that's one experience you missed."

Regards
Frank Farr

After we first contacted each other, on the internet, Frank sent me this message:

"My history in the 91st was a little messed up, Andy. I arrived at Bassingbourn in July of 1944 as a navigator on the crew of Bruce Benton, assigned to the 322nd sqdn. On our second mission, to Chartres, on Aug. 1st, (from Anderson: That was my 7th mission. We lost one of my good friends, Stevens, flying in the 324th—it was a rough day) a big chunk of flak, two or three times the size of a .45 slug, tore through my flying boot. Before it hit me it tore through the top of my navigator's table, bounced around until it tore through the heavy metal zipper on my flying boot, and into my foot. I lost a bootful of blood and missed about three weeks of action. During this time my pilot, Bruce Benton, who was a superb pilot, collapsed on the field after five missions and was sent back to the States as an instructor. In the air Bruce appeared to be a tower of strength, never raising his voice or sounding excited. However he never let off any steam, didn't drink his whiskey at the end of a mission, didn't go off to Cambridge or London carousing—nothing. So he fainted dead away one day and that was the end of combat for him. He was sent back to the States to instruct. We were assigned a pilot named Trent and I flew a couple of missions with that crew, then I was transferred to the 323rd sqdn, and assigned as navigator to Val Maghee. I flew several missions with that crew, then was assigned as navigator for the O.J. Snow crew. On the Nov. 2nd mission to Meresburg we were shot down. I finally got my chute open and ended up in a prison camp, first Stalag Luft III, and later, after the 'death march' of the winter of '44, to Stalag VII-A, at Moosburg. Like you, I've always felt very fortunate to be alive, and I'm working on my own book. We'll trade books, some day." it was good to hear from Frank. I didn't know him at the time, of course, but the few of us who are left have found each other over the internet and through our Group communication, as Frank and I did. He's written a book, "A Kriegie's Story", which will be available on Amazon in a month. I'm looking forward to reading it, and I'm sure many of you readers will be reading it, too.

But so many years had gone by when I wrote that account. So many years without a thought of the events of those days, except when I sat down to write that article. And then more years until the Palm Springs gathering, when the Air Museum there was able to locate the few of us to meet and share memories. Then one more gathering, at a Chino airshow, where we gathered after the show for a dinner together.

When I sat down at that dinner table beside a distinguished looking gentleman, shook his hand, said, "Hi. I'm Andy Anderson," I didn't realize how lucky I was. Beside me was one of the originators, one of the actual creators of the early life of that storied Group that I later became a part of, the 91st Heavy Bombardment Group. We exchanged stories, but when I began to realize the history that was embodied in the man beside me, I said, "Bert, in the past few months I've been doing what research I can into what happened in the 91st. I've been reading what I can find of the record of our missions. I've found that we were the most decorated group in the 8th Air Force. I believe we were best equipped, best trained, most skilled group in the 8th Air Force, but when I came back from the few weeks that I was missing from the group after being shot down over Ludwigshaven on September 5th, 1944, there was almost no one left that I knew. I've found some records of that time, and what I've found astonishes me. Numbers are never exact, but there were roughly 36 planes, ready for combat, assigned to a B-17 Group. During the time that I flew, from the middle of June, 1944, to September 5th, 1944, we lost 32 of our 36 planes in combat. There were several more lost in accidents, and there were planes so badly shot up that they could never fly again. They're not counted as losses, but we actually did lose 32 of our 36 planes in combat, including mine. That's quite a loss record. I know it was worse at the beginning, and you were there. What was your loss rate?" He said, "I kept pretty good records, and I've put our history on tape and put it on file. You're welcome to read those records, but I'll go home, see if I can find an answer to your question, and send it to you."

He did, and he gave me permission to share it, so I will, and then I'll get back to my personal story, because I'm alive, and to be alive I have to be the luckiest man in the world. So many men, the bravest men in the world, many far braver than I, did not live through that holocaust. I did. Bert did, and a relatively few others did, but let me start with Bert's story. This is what he sent me:

"Hi, Andy,

You asked me for information about casualties during the early months of the 91st Bomb Group's combat operational experience. Your current request reminded me that I had not responded. Sorry about that. Here is some background information about myself which will explain some choices I had to make, choices which determined my Air Force career.

    1. I graduated in 1938 from the University of Florida, BSME, and 2nd Lieutenant, FA, Res.

    2. Volunteered for active duty in March of 1941 and was assigned as battery officer with the 'integrated' (i.e. white officers from the southern states and black enlisted men from the northern states) 351st Field Artillery Regiment of the U.S. Army.

Organizationally it was a volatile ethnic mixture, and some three years later there was a disastrous battle in North Africa proving that volatility—where enlisted men fled their gun positions while under enemy fire.

    3. I could foresee that possible consequence, so I tried every avenue of escape to leave that outfit before it disintegrated. Finally the opportunity came when I was granted the opportunity to qualify as a rated Aerial Observer and then to participate in the Louisiana Maneuvers (summer, 1941). Subsequently I was assigned to the 34th Infantry Division, Camp Claiborne, Louisiana, where I was to serve as Air Office on the General Staff, with additional duty as the Army Air Corps Recruiting Officer.

    4. In the month of November, 1941, I received a letter from the Army Air Corps addressed to all reserve officers under the age of 27 who had an interest in flying, were in good health, and had good academic grades. Those officers were invited to make application for pilot training. The letter explained that Aviation cadets were being processed by the thousands, and the graduate second lieutenants were being assigned to combat groups that had very few senior officers to serve in leadership and command roles.

    5. Viewing this as an option to escape from the 351st Field Artillery Regiment, I filled out an application and submitted it.

    6. In December I received notification as to when and where I was to report for my various exams and final interview. On Dec.

20th I received orders to report to Kelly Field, Texas, to commence pilot training as a student officer. (1st Lt. F.A.) I completed training in the class of 42 G and was awarded my pilot's wings on August 5th, 1942.

Somehow we were overlooked, so after two months of fruitless search for combat training I, along with seventeen of my 2nd Lt. classmates volunteered to join the 91st Heavy Bombardment Group, which at that time had arrived at Bangor, Maine, was preparing to make the jump overseas, but was somehow short of co-pilots. I was lucky enough to be assigned as co-pilot for 2nd Lt. Don Bader, on B-17 # 24482, "Heavyweight Annihilator." That was my introduction to B-17s.

Breaking new ground with every hour in the air, and with me still learning where the landing gear controls were, we took those B-17s the Northern Route, over the cold Atlantic, with a few necessary stops along the way, to Dumbolton, England, arriving there on Oct 1, 1942."

Anderson speaking here, adding a little history. The first 91st loss occurred on Oct. 3rd, when a 401st sqdn. plane, listed only as LL, crashed in Northern Ireland on its way to Dumbolton. While the rest of the Group was finding its way to Dumbolton Colonel Wray wasted no time in locating what would be their permanent base at Bassingbourn.

American air power had yet to prove itself. The most effective formations to be flown for their own protection had not even been designed. There was a desperate need for combat training, for learning, from the veteran British fliers who had fought the Luftwaffe to a standstill in the air over Britain, the tactics to be used in defending against the battle-trained German fighters.

But there was no time. The submarines from the sub pens on the French and German coasts were devastating the supply routes from America to Britain. The 91st had time for only three brief training missions before their first bombing effort against the sub pens at Brest and St. Nazaire.

Now back to Bert's message to me.

"We flew to England, eventually, located at Bassingbourn, previously an English base, and began training for combat duty."

Anderson: Short training, indeed. They moved in at Bassingbourn on October 14, 1942. The weather was so bad that they had time for only three brief training missions, then they flew their first combat mission on Nov. 7, to hit the sub pens at Brest, France. Five of their first nine missions were flown against those sub pens, and the Eighth Air Force was just now in the process of developing the theory and practice of formation flying which would allow the concentrated firepower of many bombers to defend against the fierce fighter attacks of the Luftwaffe, who had gained experience and skill against the RAF, and against the rugged Russians, for long periods of time before the Americans arrived.

Now back to Bert's message, again.

"We flew eight of the first B-17 combat missions over occupied Europe. At first the Germans didn't know how to handle us, but it wasn't long before the anti-aircraft fire and the German fighters adjusted to us, and the fighting became fierce."

Anderson: Fierce, indeed. I'll tell the story of what happened to the Bader crew, on which Bert was flying co-pilot, a little later. I'll finish Bert's account here, first. By the time the Bader crew completed its twenty-five missions, and they did complete them, the Group had lost 38 of its 36 assigned planes. That is obviously more than 100%, but replacement crews kept coming in, so the Group was kept at full strength, even while losing what amounted to the entire Group. Now I'll let Bert finish his story.

"The German submarines were taking a terrible toll on Allied shipping, so our first effort was to knock out as much as we could of the German submarine strength. We flew our first mission against the submarine pens at Brest, France, and our ninth mission against the sub pens at St. Nazaire. By that time the German anti-aircraft gunners and fighters pilots knew what to do, so the battles became intense. On that ninth mission our # four engine was set afire by a flak hit, and our # 2 was knocked out by a fighter attack. Succeeding fighter attacks seriously wounded the pilot, Don Bader, and the bombardier, Jim Hensley. Severely damaged, we fought our way back across France, and to the middle of the English Channel, where the German fighters broke off their attacks, but not before our gunners had destroyed six of them. Don was too severely injured to fly, so I took over and brought us back to the southern tip of England. Near St. Eval I made an emergency landing on a sloping, grassy RAF fighter training field. I had been a co-pilot. There had been no time to give me the training or practice necessary to accomplish the necessary landing procedures. This was my first unassisted landing and I was rapidly coming to the end of the grassy surface, so Don, barely conscious, yelled "Ground loop, ground loop." I cut the engines, applied hard right rudder and right aileron as if I were doing a steep turn. The right wingtip dug into the ground, tossing the plane around as if we were in a sling-shot. When the dust settled I could see that we were still in what was left of an airplane. I checked to see that the rest of the crew did not have serious injuries, saw that an ambulance transported Jim and Don to the Taunton hospital, and went to make billeting arrangements in a nearby RAF facility for the remainder of the crew.

After losing my aircraft my status was reviewed by my squadron commander, Major Fishburne. He and Colonel Wray concurred that I had two choices: a. Since I had been doing double duty, serving as the 322nd squadron operations officer for the past three months, with a performance rating of 'outstanding' it was preferred that I remain in that position, but not be required to fly any more combat missions, BUT I would be required to remain in the ETO until the end of the war. Or: b. That I return to combat status as a co-pilot with Don Bader and complete my 25 missions. If successful I would then be returned to the States for re-assignment.

I was given 48 hours to make a decision. In the process of considering these choices I kept coming back to that letter from the Army Air Corps, saying it wanted me to apply for pilot training in officer grade because the Corps needed my seniority for leadership roles. So, with a heavy heart at leaving my crew, I opted for 'a' and remained as the 322nd squadron operations officer.

Don completed his 25th mission on June 28, 1943, against the sub pens at St. Nazaire. Note that he flew his first mission against the Brest pens on November 7, 1942, so the total elapsed time from the first to the last mission was six months and three weeks. Of course, much of that time he had been off flying status while recovering from battle injuries. During that time, the Group's casualties were:

a. 322 sqdn: McCormick/Zienowics, Felton, Broley, Baxley, Kahl, Brodnax.

Total: six crews b. 323 sqdn: Anderson, Bobrow, Ellis, McCarty, Rand, Biggs, Stark, Retchin, Slattery.

Total: nine crews c. 324 sqdn: Smelzer, Henderson, Brill, McClellan, Coen, Fischer, Koll, Miller

Total: eight crews d. 401 sqdn: Corson, English, Bloodgood, Smith, Swais, O'Neil, Beasley, Walker, Stoffel, Wilson, Lindsey, Fountain, Brown

Total: thirteen crews

Total Group combat losses---36 crews

When you realize that the original squadron strength was nine aircraft, the above date show that we lost them all in that period of time. In Brent Perkins' (Director of the Memphis Belle Memorial Association) book, he presented a similar record of what happened to each of the 36 B-17s that made that trans-Atlantic crossing. I hope this answers your questions.

My best regards, Bert."

Anderson, again.

Bert didn't count the ship that was lost on the way over, LL. I would add that. So by the time Don Bolton completed his 25th mission and was eligible to return home to the "Zone of the Interior" Bert lists 36, plus the one. The Group records list two other combat losses, so during Bolton's flight time the Group lost 39 planes and crews. Out of 36 assigned. That's what? About 110 percent? Pretty heavy. Of course those planes and crews were replaced as soon as possible, so by the time I began to fly, in June of 1944, the Group strength of 36 had been resumed, more than once. And we lost 32 planes and crews while I was flying. They were replaced as they were lost, of course, but only through this research have I been able to understand why, when I returned to the Group a little more than a month after I had been shot down, I recognized so few faces.

Bert's account describes some of the very first missions flown by the 8th Air Force, often with the 91st in the lead. Remember, the 91st flew its first combat mission against the sub pens at Brest, on the French coast, on November 7th. Bert notes that, including that mission to Brest, five of those first nine missions were flown against sub pen targets. On their 9th mission, the Group's 13th, to St. Nazaire, Bader's plane and crew were almost destroyed, so severely damaged that it was some time before they flew again, but the 91st did not stop attacking. During the rest of 1942, November and December, they kept flying missions. By the end of the year they had already lost seven planes and crews. By the end of April the group had lost 16 more. That's 23 planes and crews in a period of four months. By the end of the 7th month the 91st had lost 37 planes and crews.

That's one more than the entire group in the first seven months of combat. A year and a half later, in the roughly ten weeks that my crew flew, the 91st lost 32 planes and crews. That would make it seem that survival rates increased as the war went on. That was not true, however. The first months of American bomber combat were by far the most difficult. The first Groups in combat had to learn as they flew, and their heavy losses reflected how much they had to learn. By the time my crew arrived at Bassingbourn, the 91st base, a year and a half later, the Air Corps, soon to be renamed the Air Force, had learned how much tight formation flying focused fire power, which formations presented the strongest deterrent to German fighters, which continental ground areas had the heaviest concentration of anti-aircraft guns, (and thus were to be avoided enroute to bombing targets), gunners were better trained, an improved model of the B-17 had arrived, with nose guns installed, the lack of which was a near fatal defect in the earlier models, some training, a minimum, admittedly, but some training could be given in survival tactics for those crews who survived the initial destruction of their planes—(by bailing out, etc.)

Despite all of this, the loss rate through my months in combat remained close to the rate of the early months. The Germans brought their best fighter pilots, some of whom had the incredible number of near 200 kills, back from the Russian Front to protect their munitions and aircraft factories, which we were just as desperately trying to destroy. And we got to them just in time. In late 1942 a German four engine ME 264 plane took its first flight. This aircraft, the "Amerika Bomber" could carry two tons of bombs 9000 miles. A six engine Ju 200 actually made a flight to New York, where it took photographs of potential targets, and back. However, only 41 Ju

290s were built and they were never put to use as bombers. The Me 264 was designed as a bomber, and then, with the introduction of the two-engine fighter, the Me 262, in 1944, the 264 was converted from a prop to a jet aircraft. This increased its speed from 373 to 500 miles per hour. At this speed, defensive armament and gunners could be dispensed with. But that Ju 290 flight to New York did not go unnoticed. British code-breakers learned about the flight from secret German messages. For some reason they waited several months to tell the Americans about it, but when they did we sent bombers to destroy the factories producing the Me 264. They did and because of the intensive bombing by the 8th Air Force, the Germans were not able to muster the resources to rebuild it, or to build another. Tentative plans had been made to send 290s with "buzz bombs" attached under their wings to hit Boston or New York. A "buzz bomb" was a small pilotless plane filled with explosives, which devastated British cities and could have sent New York and Boston into a tailspin of terror. Fortunately, the 'buzz bombs' never arrived.

In late July and early August, 1944, the 8th Air Force, with the 91st in the lead, bombed Peenemunde and Nuernburg, where jet airplane experimentation and production were being carried out, and where jet fighter production was under way. We knew it was important stuff because of the intensive briefings we got before the missions, but no one ever told us why it was important. I had to wait until 2002, when I was reading everything I could find about WW II for this writing, to find, in a book, "Dirty Little Secrets Of World War II," the information about the German jet production, and I don't know where I picked up the knowledge of the German effort at an Atomic Bomb, or if we demolished any of that with our bombing of Peenamunde. I believe we did, and our bombing of the Romanian oil fields at Ploesti and the ball-bearing plants at Schweinfurt did tremendous damage to the German war materiel production. Those raids heavily depleted the 8th Air Force, but the 91st continued to lead the way in the Allies' effort to destroy both the German Air Force and the German war materiel production capability.

Other Groups, which had begun to flow into England from the "Zone of the Interior," however, had similar, often heavier losses. A debate began, in both the 8th and the War Department headquarters as to whether the war effort and the nation could afford this loss of such a large percentage of one of the most able and skilled divisions of our armed forces. It must be kept in mind that the German submarine armada was destroying much of the war capability which the United States was supplying to the Allies with its freight supply line, but the combined Allied navies were learning better how to fight the subs, too. Where should our strengths be concentrated, and where should a greater effort be made to reduce our losses?

As the anti-submarine strength and skills of our naval forces grew stronger, the destructive power of our heavy bomber force began to be shifted to destroying the materiel resources of Hitler's war machine. The bombing of the sub pens continued, but the major destructive effort of the heavy bombers began to be shifted to destroying the war materiel capacity of the German Homeland. Later examination revealed that this was a wise decision. The Germans had invested a huge portion of their resources in constructing and defending the submarine infrastructure on the French coast. After the German surrender it was found that more then 3,000 artillery pieces and 5,000 coast artillerymen were engaged in the defense of Lorient. This was more than five times the artillery that rained death on the G. I.s who stormed ashore at Omaha Beach. In addition, hundreds of Focke-Wulf and Messerschmitt fighters were constantly available to protect those sub pens from the American bombers. For months after the surrender of the French forces in the Compiegne Forest, the submarines, which were largely cared for at the sub pens on the French coast, were the best offensive weapon the German High Command possessed. Immediately after that surrender a train left Wilhelmshaven, Germany, headed for the Brittany coast, Lorient, and Brest, then to St. Nazaire, Pallice, and Bordeaux. With this support and supply available, the U-boat offensive moved to a new level. (By late 1940 the U-boat offensive had moved to a new level.) The U-boat construction in Germany had increased to 30 a month. The war, for Germany, seemed won. There appeared to be no threat from the United States. In 1940 the American army was ranked 18th in the world, just behind Holland's. The U-boats even began to rule the American coasts. Jerome O'Conner, in an article in the July, 2002, issue of "World War II Magazine" noted that an alarmed American

Chief of Staff, George Marshall, wrote to Naval Commander-in-Chief Ernest J. King, on July 19, 1942, that:

"I am fearful that another month or two of this will so cripple our means of transport that we will be unable to bring sufficient men and planes to bear against the enemy " (to ever defeat him.) Naval historian Samuel Eliot Morrison said that "It was as much a national disaster as if sabateurs had destroyed half a dozen of our biggest war plants."

Before the end of March, 1942, the submarine fleet had sunk 216 merchant ships, most of them tankers. After sinking a tanker off the eastern American coast in 1942, German sub U-123 reported to submarine command at Lorient how clearly the lights of Coney Island illuminated the target.

France was defeated. Britain was lying almost incapacitated. A somnolent United States was only beginning to move. Then one of the miracles of the Allied war effort occurred. Germany had created a code that it regarded as unbreakable, and named it 'Enigma'. With an enormous massing of brainpower in the warrens of the British establishment, 'Ultra," a process to break the German "Enigma' was created. The Germans believed their code could never be broken and continued to use it throughout the war, but by 1943, 3000 coded 'Enigma' messages were being decoded each day at Bleachley Park, outside London, by 12,000 British code-breakers. This achievement reversed the course of the Battle of the Atlantic. 'Ultra' was the first factor in the sinking of almost the entire U-boat fleet. The Americans were not informed of these achievements, but they did know of the disastrous effect of the U-boats on the Allied supply lines, so as they shifted the emphasis of their bombing to the destruction of the German industrial base and air power, they returned, intermittently, to the bombing of the German sub pens. We hit those pens hard, with tremendous amounts of explosives, and we knew our bombing was accurate, because we took pictures of the bomb patterns. What we didn't know was the tremendous amount of skill, materiel, and effort which went into the building of those submarine resources. When the Germans finished the conquest of France they went right to work on creating a support base on the French coasts for their submarines. They put more concrete into those pens, underground and hidden, than we had put into our Boulder (later Hoover) Dam. And they had more heavy guns protecting them, pointing up, than they had defending the beaches when the invasion eventually did take place. More than two months after the invasion date, on August 8th, the 91st flew a mission aimed at destroying ammunition dumps and a concentration of German ground troops. The mission target was listed as Caen, but we actually dropped on the ammo dumps and sub fortifications at Brest. We dropped from 25,000 feet that day, and it wasn't high enough. We lost one of our best planes, Chow Hound, from the 322nd, with a good friend of mine as pilot. That was my 9th mission, number 212 for the 91st, and it came at a particularly hard time for us. On July 20th, on a mission to Leipzig, the 91st lost eight planes, three from the 322nd. We'd have been among them, but we were stood down. Just our crew. Didn't know why, but we were glad to be alive. A few days after the Caen mission, on August 16th, on a mission to an airfield at Halle, the 91st lost six planes, the whole 324th squadron. The whole 322nd was stood down that day, again, no reason, except that the 322 had been hit pretty hard at Leipzig and squadrons which had been badly hurt were often stood down the next mission or two to recover, physically and emotionally, and the day before, on the 15th, we'd flown a particularly rough mission to hit a German airdrome at Ostheim, just four miles from Cologne. Surprisingly, the 91st didn't lose any planes at Ostheim, but the flak was heavy and a number of ships took severe damage. We flew Choo Choo Lady and we came home with so much damage that it was a miracle we made it back. That "Lady" is a tough old girl. She really wasn't airworthy to bring us back, but she did, and we were grateful. So many holes we didn't try to count them. A number of men killed in other planes. Bandits hit the group behind us hard. Hammer led the low group (us) and he did a good job, except he took us into the prop wash of the lead group on the bomb run and we couldn't hold formation. Turned out that wasn't a bad thing, though. The German gunners somehow had our number, and they put heavy flak right where we would have been if we hadn't been blown off by the prop wash. The hand of God held us today. Time after time I watched the flak line move toward us and braced for a hit, but each time it hesitated and moved on. Nobody griped at Hammer at the debriefing.

Tom was really beat---7 1/2 hour trip, five hours on oxygen, so I did the landing. So tired I bounced her in, but lucky to get in at all. Brakes shot out, little pressure, so I damn near ran out of runway before I could stop her. Both of us on the brakes weren't enough. Throttle still off a couple of inches. Seemed silly to put that on the Form I A when we were so full of holes, but the crew were OK, and the 'off' throttle made tight formation flying tough, so I wrote it up. It'll be fixed. Ground crews get right on the problems. Fighters hit most of the other groups, today, but none on us, so Shockley had time, from the tail, to watch the bomb hits. He said they strung right across the field and into the hangers, then he was "too damn scared" (his words at debriefing) to watch any more. I like Choo Choo, but she floats, and brakes mostly gone didn't help any.

Lost my roommate, Will Keck, on the Leipzig mission. Good guy. We came in in the same group. I didn't know him in Louisiana, but we were pretty busy, there. His crew was "55". We were "45". New guy not the same. They should let us room with our own crew. Our crew is still together, but most of my other friends are gone. My God, we've lost 31 planes while I've been flying. That's almost the whole Group.

And I was next. But I didn't mean to get into my missions, yet. First I need to tell you about the 91st, and how I got here. And flying. Flying. There is nothing else like it. Long after I learned to fly, after I'd done most of my university work, and was teaching English (among other things) at Manual Arts High in Los Angeles, I found these words, written by an Englishman, John Gillespie Magee, Jr. They say, better than I, how I felt about flying as I was learning:

"Oh, I have slipped the surly bonds of earth
And danced the skies on laughter silvered wings.
Sunward I've climbed and joined the tumbling mirth
Of sun-split clouds—and done a hundred things
You have not dreamed of—wheeled and soared and swung
High in the sun-lit silence. Hov'ring there
I've chased the shouting wind along
And flung my eager craft through footless halls of air.
Up, up the long delirious burning blue
And, while with silent, lifting mind I've trod

The high untrespassed sanctity of space,
Put out my hand, and touched the face of God.

The day I soloed, in that sturdy old PT-17 biplane, was the day I joined John McGee, "High in the sunlit silence. Hov'ring there, chasing the shouting wind, up, up the delirious burning blue, through footless halls of air."

My grizzled instructor (they had recruited old timers to teach us fresh but raw young recruits to fly) had taken me out to the airplane. I had never been near an airplane, before. He said, "You been in one of these, son?"

I said, "No, sir." He said, "Well climb in. We may as well begin."

I climbed into the front seat. He showed me how to fasten the safety belt, then he climbed into the rear seat. He turned on the switch, motioned to the ground man to turn over the prop until the engine caught, and taxied out onto the runway. At the end of the runway he stopped, ran up the engine to check the mags, turned onto the runway and took off. He flew out of the pattern (I had no idea what a flight pattern was), climbed up a couple of thousand feet and turned the plane over. I hung there from my safety belt, scared stiff, hanging onto the control stick for dear life. I don't know how he turned that plane back over, with me frozen to the stick, but he did, then took it back, showed me how to enter the flight pattern, landed, and said, "Now, that wasn't too bad, was it?" I was still blue with fright, but I managed to say "No, sir." So he said, "OK, let's do it again." So we did, with him this time explaining each procedure as we went through it. He had me follow through on the stick and rudder as he shot landings, then did the same as we went through stalls, necessary because the only really vital skill necessary in learning to fly is to bring the plane in on the landing approach so that the final round-out is completed as the plane stalls out just as the wheels touch the runway. We practiced doing stalls in the air until I could identify the instant when the stall was about to take place, and then on the approach could touch the plane down at that instant and taxi on down the runway. Every pilot will remember when he reached that moment. It was a high spot in our lives. It is not a matter of intelligence. Some students, far brighter than I, simply could not reach that "feel", so they were "washed out" and went to Navigation, Bombardier, or Gunnery school. Those of you who do a great deal of flying, now, will be able to identify the instant that the airplane approaches the runway when the pilot rounds out the glide so that the plane stalls out just as the wheels touch. That will happen each time a plane lands if the pilot is as skillful as he (or she) should be. The engines on today's planes are so powerful that a touch of the throttle can cover up the occasional slight lapse of a pilot's skill or judgment. I still chuckle when I feel that happen. Now back to my story.

I was fortunate, indeed, in my primary instructor. From being a kid just out of high school, who'd never been near an airplane, I was led through the multitude of skills necessary to approach being a pilot. He taught me how to go into and break out of a spin, to snap roll and slow roll, and all of the small skills necessary to become an accomplished pilot, so that when he climbed out of his cockpit one day, far sooner than I thought he should, waved me on down the runway, and watched as I came around and landed, then shot landings the rest of the morning, I could, with John Magee, "slip the surly bonds of earth" and be free in the sky to put my wing in the edge of a cloud, fly around it, wing over and go home—to an afternoon of flight school. We learned flight theory as we put it into practice. We learned Morse code as the control tower shot signals at us as they gave us instructions in the air—there were no radios in the PTs. (primary trainers.) Sometime in that first week of solo practice I got so involved with practicing stalls that I forgot to keep a close watch on the ground, and when I was ready to go back to the field and shoot more landings I didn't know where it was. I could see two rivers and lots of green fields, but I had no idea where the flight base was. I almost panicked. The day before, an upper classman had become lost, as I was, and ended up in Florida, where he landed on a strange field just as he ran out of gas. He was made fun of by our instructors and laughed at by us lower classmen, and now here I was in the same situation. Fortunately, just as I was about to give way to despair, a classmate flew by on his way back to the base (he knew where it was). He waved at me as he went by, so I followed him home, landed, wiped off the sweat, and took off again to practice more landings. I never got lost again.

And we didn't regret the hours we spent sitting on a bench practicing the morse code that few of us would ever use again, but had to be learned for the few times it would be used---including flying the radio beam in those days, which was an A (.-) on one side, and a -. (N) on the other. Later, in Advanced flight school, we learned to fly down the center of the beam to wherever we were headed, but the only place I remember using it was in the Link Trainer, where we practiced instrument flying until we flew our plane on instruments as easily as we walked down the street. I'll digress for a moment to say that if John Jr. (Kennedy) had been trained thoroughly enough to believe and fly his instruments, he would be alive today, and we would quite probably have a different national leadership.

I'm not here to teach you the curriculum of the three levels of flight school all of the Air Force pilots of those days went through, however. We all went to Pre-flight, where we were sorted out, assigned to specialty training (pilot, navigator, or bombardier), then trained in that specialty until we were judged ready to enter the real world of combat or other service. For pilots, that training consisted of Primary Flight School, where we learned the basics of flight and the practical knowledge necessary to go with those basics: flight theory, basic mechanics, meteorology, navigation, basic weapon handling, etc. The list could go on and on. We covered a condensed version of what would later become the three year Air Force Academy curriculum in less than a year. There was no respite and no mercy, and we asked for none. Those who could not absorb the learning required, at the rate demanded, simply disappeared, sent to another kind of training or back to the infantry. The intellectual level required was high, the physical training rigorous, and the dedication focus demanding. A large percentage of those who entered flight training never completed it. They 'washed out' and were sent elsewhere. There was no feeling of 'eliteness,' however. We all knew that those who left us and went elsewhere for training were, in many ways, as good, or better men than we, but we were lucky enough to be able to achieve on a scale which allowed us to complete our chosen training and become Air Force Officers and soon to be combatants. After Primary Flight School we went to Basic, then to Advanced flight schools, which were simply continuations, on a more advanced level, and in more advanced airplanes, of the training we had begun in 'Primary.' Graduates from West Point and from university ROTCs who wanted to fly joined us, went through the same training and were assigned, with us, to various further training, as we were. They lived a little better because they were already second lieutenants, but they were members of our class in every other way. Two second lieutenants, recent graduates from West Point, joined our Primary class in our Mississippi flight school. I knew them a bit because one of them was a runner, and he and I competed in our daily five mile runs. We always ended up together in the stretch, far ahead of the large group, who didn't feel the need to compete, as he and I did. A third cadet, from Glendale, Bob Free, and I almost always finished first in our runs. The lieutenant couldn't quite match Bob and me, and he got a little testy at times. We soloed at about the same time and often did our solo practicing in the same general air space. One of the first things we learned in the air was how to put our plane in and out of a spin, because a stall is the immediate preceeder of a spin and either the stall or the spin can cost the pilot's life if it happens on the approach to a landing. We were all young, and vigorous almost beyond measure so we fiddled with the rules, occasionally. One of the rules was that you never begin a spin without enough air beneath you to assure you of coming out of the spin safely. I watched the lieutenant fiddle with that rule, one day, as he showed those of us near him how close to the ground he could come before pulling out of his spin. This day he didn't make it. He spun in, losing his life, and what was perhaps even more valuable, his airplane. There weren't enough of those precious PT-17s and each one destroyed was as much a tragedy as the loss of the pilot in it.

I've strayed. This story began as the story of the 91st Heavy bombardment Group and of my small part in it. Let me get back to some of the story of the 91st, so I can get to how I became a part of it.

Perhaps the most important mission the 91st ever flew was the mission to Hamm, the first really deep penetration of the German homeland by the 8th Air Force, on March 4, 1943. Bert Humphries has told you, here, of his entry into the 91st, of his 9th mission, which was # 13 for the 91st, and of the result of it for him. He then became operations officer for the 322 squadron and flew no more missions, but the 91st continued to fly and to learn. By that 13th mission, which was Bert's last, the leaders of the 8th Air Force (as it soon became known) became aware of how important the massing of 50 calibre machine gun fire was to the defense of each individual airplane of the group. Commanders and pilots in the Group quickly became skilled in formation flying and bombing missions. Raids were henceforth conducted in Group formation, with the groups eventually formed into Wings (three or more Groups) so that the massed firepower of a group was a formidable obstacle to the growingly fierce German fighter attacks. The downside of tight formation flying was that it made us, flying close together and unable to change position in the formation, a better target for the German ground batteries, which achieved incredible accuracy in a very brief time.

The Germans developed, and distributed to their pilots, sketches of the firing range of each of the B-17's (and B-24's) machine guns, and the German pilots became very skillful at penetrating into the most vulnerable areas of the big bombers, delivering their lethal blows in the least protected and most effective (for them) areas.

On December 30th, the 91st flew its twelfth mission. This one was to the sub pens at St. Lorient. They lost their seventh (six in combat) plane, Short Snorter. The formation flying was getting better. The massing of machine gun fire, to some extent, held off the German fighter attacks, but it was no protection against the flak, and the flak umbrella over the sub pen areas was becoming massive. They flew their 13th mission against the sub pens at St. Nazaire and lost their eighth plane and crew, Panhandle Dogie. Only the navigator, Lt. J.R. Roten, survived to live in a prison camp until the end of the war. The subsequent missions were flown largely against sub pens, until the 4th of March. During those eight missions we lost five more planes and crews, three from the 323 and two from the 401st. Ordinarily the Group flew with a strength of 27 planes, if that many were in flying condition, so by the time the March 4 mission was over (we lost 4 planes and crews) we had lost 16 of our 36 planes—16 out of a normal flying strength of 27. Whew! In fourteen weeks the Group had lost nearly half of its total strength. And other Groups had similar losses. No wonder a debate began at the various headquarters. Could we afford to lose planes and crews at that rate? What must we do, if it were possible to do anything, to make such a loss rate worthwhile?

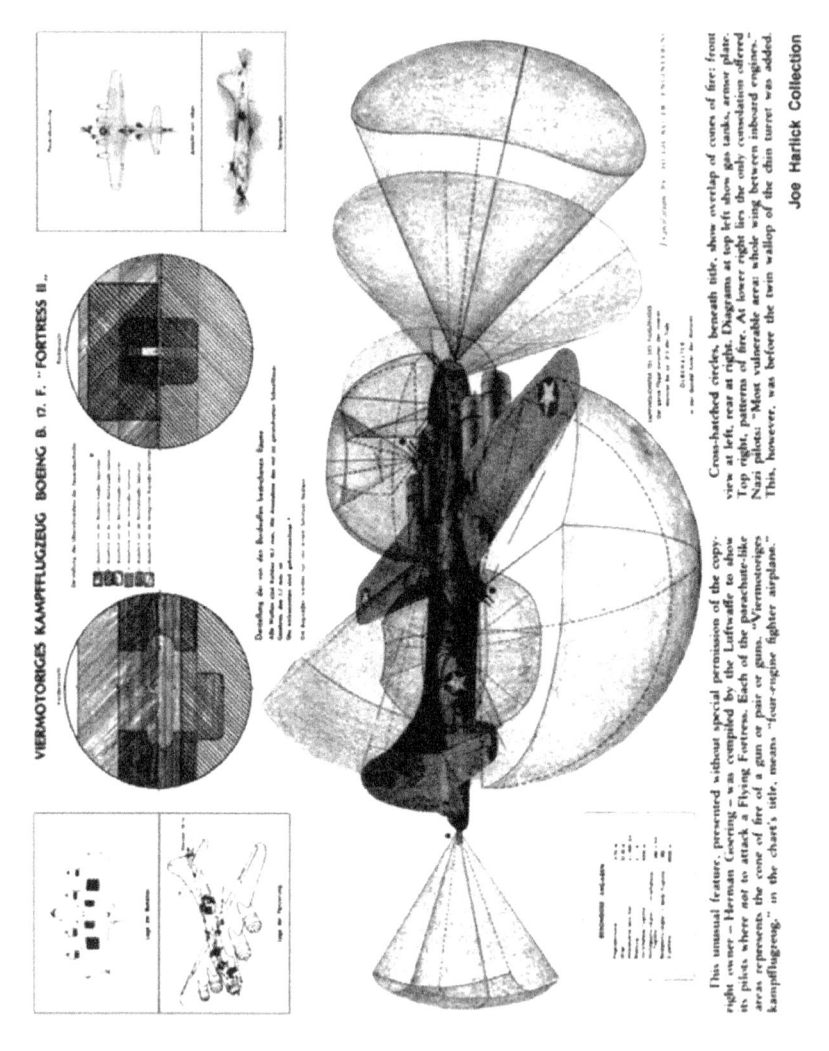

Figure: German Luftwaffe diagram "Viermotoriges Kampfflugzeug Boeing B. 17. F. — 'Fortress II'" showing fields of fire and vulnerable areas of the B-17. Joe Harlick Collection.

Cross-hatched circles, beneath title, show overlap of cones of fire: front view at left, rear at right. Diagrams at top left show gas tanks, armor plate, etc. at pilots where not to attack a Flying Fortress. Each of the parachute-like areas represents the cone of fire of a gun or pair of guns. "Viermotoriges kampfflugzeug," in the chart's title, means "four-engine fighter airplane."

This unusual feature, prevented without special permission of the copyright owner — Herman Goering — was compiled by the Luftwaffe to show its pilots where not to attack a Flying Fortress. Top right, patterns of fire. At lower right lies the only consolation offered Nazi pilots: "Most vulnerable areas while wing between inboard engines." This, however, was before the twin wallop of the chin turret was added.

While those discussions are taking place, let me share with you what happened on those missions subsequent to that 13th mission to St. Nazaire. On January 13th the 91st hit the rail yards at Lille. No losses. On January 23, the 15th mission, it was back to the sub pens at St. Lorient.—no losses. On January 27th they hit the docks at Wilhelmshaven, no losses, but let me add a comment. Anti-aircraft guns, flak guns, were being added to the defense of those vital submarine bases all of the time. Eventually there were more than twice as many 98 and 105 millimeter guns defending those sub bases as were used to defend the beaches during the Normandy invasion a year and a half later. The submarines, used to destroy the supplies and the will of the Allies, were the most powerful weapon, both offensive and defensive, that the Nazis possessed.

SECRET

APPENDIX D
Direction of Attacks and Hits on B-17's
by Enemy Fighters

July - November 1943

The frequency with which our bombers have been attacked and hit, from each direction, and the relative effectiveness of our defensive gunfire against enemy fighter attacks from various directions, can be inferred from the following:

The data on hits are taken from a tally of the direction from which enemy cannon fire and small calibre machine gun fire entered the exterior surfaces of heavy bombers, as reported in ORS forms between July and November 1943.

Since these reports of encounters are connected with claims, and often no reports are made when no claims are made, the frequency of "attack" from each direction may more nearly represent the frequency with which enemy fighters, <u>which were hit</u> by our defensive fire, attacked from each direction. Any directions from which they attack, but are faced by inferior defensive fire, may be understated. However, our relative advantage or disadvantage against enemy fighter attacks from any direction can be gauged by the ratio between reported "attacks" and hits from that direction.

Of course, these attack figures represent only those B-17s that returned home. -Editor

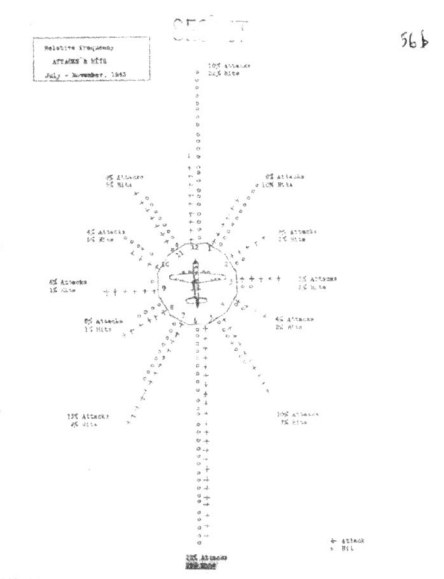

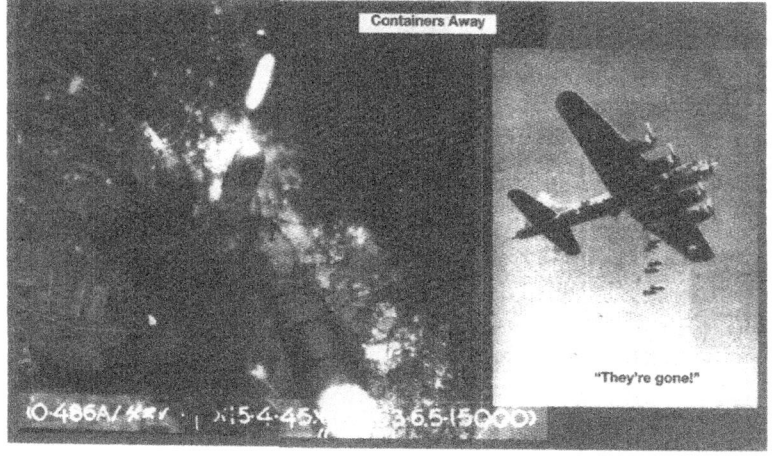

"Containers Away"

"They're gone!"

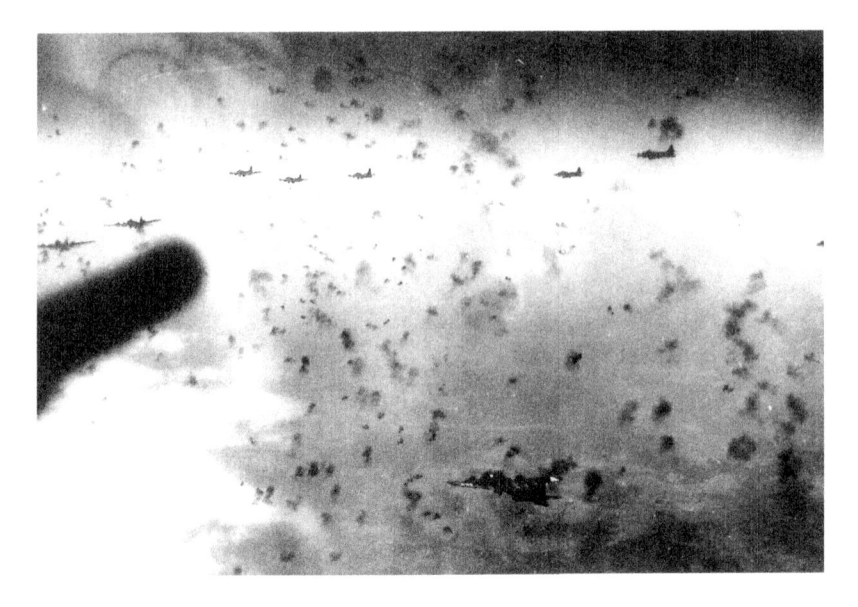

B-17s flying through a flak barrage

Remember the remark of the American general, who said, in effect, "Much more of this and we'll not be able to supply the armies which we will need for the invasion of 'Festung Europa'." At one time the German submarine production level approached thirty a month. If this rate had continued, the Allied supply route would have been totally disrupted and the German conquest of the Western World would have been complete.

Fortunately, this did not happen. Several circumstances combined so that the Allies were able to break the German code, "Enigma," with their own code weapon, "Ultra." This was accomplished through a combination of the efforts of hundreds of code breakers working in London, and the unbelievably fortunate capture of parts of the "Enigma" code books from captured German submarines, so that during the latter part of the war the Allies were able to read the directions given to the German submarines and achieve a high rate of submarine destruction. The communication level between the British and the Americans, despite their obvious dependence upon one another, was not always the best, so the Americans were not immediately aware of the code successes of the British, but they were aware that, if an eventual invasion were to succeed, German production of war material must be impeded, so the American destructive effort, with their powerful warplanes, gradually shifted from submarine destruction and interdiction to land weapon and supply destruction and interdiction. At this they were eventually eminently successful, with the 91st Heavy Bombardment Group often leading the way. You have read how the 91st was formed, how it made its way to Europe, picking up needed pilots, crews, and skills along the way. Very few of that initial group survived. That survival rate, of planes and crews, was three to five percent. I put that in words rather than in numbers so that there is no mistaking the figures. You have already read that of the initial group of 36 planes in our group, 38 were lost in combat. That figure of more than 100 % was possible because, as a plane was lost or disabled, it was replaced, so that the usable flight strength of a Heavy Combat Group remained at or near 36 airplanes. The 91st was not unique in its skills, its losses, its awards, its history, but I was a part of it and its story is the only story I can tell. That is why I am sharing this with you. I have begun to tell this story many times. Each time it has been too difficult, emotionally, for me to complete, but this time I will complete it, at least those parts of it that I am willing to tell. Most of the story will be my own, but since my combat experiences ended after my fifteenth mission, when we were shot down, I will include the stories of some of my comrades-in arms of those days—most of whom I did not know at the time, but have come to know through computer and other communications as these means have become available.

I began by telling you that not many of us survived, and that is true. Of that initial group of 36 planes and crews, 38 were destroyed in combat. That number, as you have been told, is more than 100% because as a plane and crew were shot down or destroyed, another would be sent in from the busy factories in the "Zone of the Interior" (the United States) to replace it. And men from the many training schools in the States were sent to replace those of us who were lost, one way or another.

That initial group began flying in late 1942. The combat loss rate was high. Few of the original flight personnel remained when the combat flying was ended in 1945. they either died or rotated back to the states, but most of the ground crew personnel remained through most of the war years—and we flyers owed so much to them. I have seen many a crew chief sitting beside his bicycle waiting for the planes to return from a mission, and turning away with tears on his cheeks when his plane did not return. Most ground crews were assigned to one ship, which they serviced and maintained as long as it was in service. And they became attached to the crews that flew the ships. How they maintained their stability and even sanity when their ship did not return is beyond me. And many of them lost crew after crew. It was hard, indeed. Winston Churchill tells, in a speech or writing which I will include, here, how difficult it was for him when a man he was fond of joined the British Air Force and did not return from a mission. Our ground crews went through the same emotional trauma time after time. I don't know how they survived it.

Of those who flew, Winston Churchill, in his later writing, said:

"We need to pay our tribute of respect and admiration to the officers and men who fought and died in this fearful battle of the air, the like of which had never before been known, or even, with any precision, imagined. The moral test to which the crew of a bomber was subjected reached the limits of human valor and sacrifice. Here chance was carried to its most extreme and violent degree above all else. There was a rule that no one should go on more than thirty raids without a break. But many who entered on their last dozen wild adventures felt that the odds against them were increasing. How can one be lucky thirty times running in a world of averages and machinery?

Detective-Constable McSweeney, one of the Scotland Yard officers who looked after me in the early days of the war, was determined to fight in a bomber. I saw him several times during his training and his fighting. One day, gay and jaunty as ever, but with a thoughtful look, he said, "My next will be my twenty-ninth." It was his last. Not only our hearts and admiration, but our minds in strong comprehension of those ordeals must go out to these heroic men whose duty to their country and their cause sustained them in superhuman trials.

I have mentioned facts like, "The Americans had sixty of their large fortress aircraft destroyed out of 291 on that mission," and, on another occasion, "Out of 795 aircraft sent by the British Bomber Command against Nuremburg, 94 did not return."

The American Fortresses carried a crew of ten men, and the British night bombers, seven. Here we have, each time, so many of these skilled, highly trained warriors lost in an hour. This was, indeed, trial by fire. In the British and American bombing of Germany and Italy during the war, the casualties were over a hundred and forty thousand. In the period with which this chapter deals, there were more British and American casualties than were killed and wounded in the great operation of crossing the Channel. These heroes never flinched or failed. It is to their devotion that, in no small measure, we owe our victory. Let us give them our salute."

And there is another Churchill speech that every person in the present-day free world should be familiar with. It was delivered to the House of Commons on the eve of the greatest German victory and Allied defeat. Churchill said,

"What General Weygand has called "The Battle of France" is over. The "Battle of Britain" is about to begin. Upon this battle depends the survival of Christian civilization. Upon it depends our own British life and the long continuity of our institutions and our Empire. The whole fury and might of the enemy must very soon be turned on us. Hitler knows that he must break us in this Island or lose the war. If we can stand up to him, all Europe may be free and the life of the world may move forward into broad, sunlit uplands.

But if we fail, then the whole world, including the United States, including all that we have known and cared for, will sink into the abyss of a new Dark Age made more sinister, and perhaps more protracted, by the lights of perverted science. Let us, therefore, brace ourselves to our duties, and so bear ourselves that, if the British Empire and its Commonwealth last for a thousand years, men will still say, "This was their finest hour."

Immediately following the German surrender, in 1945, our own General Eisenhower expressed a similar feeling to a wider group, our entire armed forces. This is what he said, in what was entitled "VICTORY ORDER OF THE DAY"

"Men and women of the Allied Expeditionary Forces: The crusade on which we embarked in the early summer of 1944 has reached a glorious conclusion. It is my privilege, in the name of all nations represented in this theatre of war, to commend each of you for valiant performance of duty. Though these words are feeble, they come from the bottom of a heart overflowing with pride in your loyal service and admiration for you as warriors. Your accomplishments at sea, in the air, on the ground and in the field of supply have astonished the world.

Even before the final week of conflict you had put 5,000,000 of the enemy permanently out of the war. You have taken in stride military tasks so difficult as to be classed by many doubters as impossible. You have confused, defeated, and destroyed your savagely fighting foe. On the road to victory you have endured every obstacle ingenuity and desperation could throw into your path. You did not pause until our front was firmly joined up with the great Red army coming form the East, and other Allied forces, coming from the South. Full victory in Europe has been attained. Working and fighting together in a single and indestructible partnership, you have achieved a perfection of air, ground and naval power that will stand as a model in our time. The route you have traveled, through hundreds of miles, is marked by the graves of former comrades. From them has been exacted the ultimate sacrifice. Blood of many nations, American, Canadian, British, French, Polish and others has helped gain the victory. Each of the fallen died as a member of the team to which you belong, bound together by a common love of liberty and refusal to submit to enslavement. No monument of stone, no memorial, of whatever magnitude, could so well express our respect and veneration for their sacrifice as would perpetuation of the spirit of comradeship in which they died. As we celebrate Victory in Europe let us remind ourselves that our common problems of the immediate and distant future can best be solved in the conceptions of cooperation and devotion to the cause of human freedom as have made this Expeditionary Force such a mighty engine of righteous destruction. Let us have no part in the profitless quarrels in which other men will so inevitably engage as to which country, what service won the European War. Every man, every woman, of every nation here represented has served according to his or her ability, and the efforts of each have contributed to the outcome. This we shall remember, and in doing so we shall be revering each honored grave and be sending comfort to the loved ones of comrades who could not live to see this day."

Inspiring words from Ike.

Let me look at those early missions flown by the 91st, however, so I can then get to more personal records and memories.

I've listed the Group's first sixteen missions and their casualties, and that's almost enough before I begin more detailed stories, but let me cover five more before I come to a mission that, in the judgment of many historians, and of us who were involved, had such an impact on the war itself that it was pivotal in the subsequent history and conduct of that conflict.

On February 4th, 1943, on a mission to Emden, the 91st lost two more planes, Texas Bronco and Pennsylvania Polka, and their crews. That was their 17th mission. The eighteenth mission, to Hamm, a railroad marshalling yard and center, was aborted, but credit for the mission was given because the abort was not called until the group had penetrated into the continent so far that considerable damage was caused by flak. The abort was called because the cloud cover had become so heavy over the target that there was no hope of bombing accurately because we couldn't see where our bombs were going, and it was always American policy to bomb only military targets, not civilian populations or cities with no military significance. The Group brought their bombs home, unused, that day.

Three earlier scheduled missions, to destroy the vital rail marshaling yards at Hamm, deep into Germany, had been cancelled or aborted due to heavy cloud cover over all of Europe. The nineteenth mission, to St. Nazaire, on February 16th, the twentieth, on February 26th, to Wilhelmshaven, and the twenty-first, to the sub pens at Brest, on the 27th, were all aimed at damaging the efficiency of the submarines, which were still destroying the Allied Merchant Marine Supply fleet at a disastrous rate. We lost two more planes on that 20th mission, Short Snorter and Kickapoo. The loss rate had begun to appear unbearable. With the four planes we were to lose on the next mission, to Hamm, we had lost sixteen of our airplanes and their crews in combat in a relatively short time. With the several planes that had been lost or disabled by misfortune or accident (not combat) we had lost more than half of the total Group strength—in a period of four months. If losses continued at that rate, and there was no prospect that they would not, the entire combat group would have been lost in a period of eight months. And, as a matter of fact, in a little more than another month, by April 17th, we would have lost eight more ships and crews. My God!! That's the entire group. On most missions one squadron, usually the one hurt the worst on the last mission, was rested, stood down, which means most missions were flown with 27 planes, which was a little more than we had lost by April 17th. Other groups had similar losses. The mortality rate was almost unbelievable. Fighter losses were not that staggering because at that time we had no fighters with range enough to accompany our bombers deep into Europe, where most of our losses were occurring—so since they weren't there, they couldn't be shot down.

The British had had similar losses, and it was more than they could withstand. They abandoned daylight bombing and concentrated on night bombing, where their accuracy (because they couldn't see their targets) was questionable, but their losses were not so great.

What to do? German subs were destroying American freighters almost off the American coast—freighters loaded with supplies necessary not only for British survival, but for the potential invasion and freeing of Nazi occupied Europe. If those supplies, and eventually soldiers, could not reach England, the Nazi occupation of Europe could continue indefinitely, a horrendous prospect.

Two other things occurred in mid 1943 which portended disaster for the Allied war effort. The first was the realization, partly through information from scientists who had defected from Germany, that the German effort to develop a weapon of tremendous mass destruction, an atom bomb, was nearing completion. One of the final components was the construction of a 'heavy water' plant near the Norwegian town of Rjuken, ninety miles west of the Norwegian capitol of Oslo. Germany had conquered and occupied Norway in 1940, and installed a cooperative government headed by a Norwegian who was willing to work with them named Quisling. The word has survived to this day as a synonym for traitor and traitorous actions. The vast majority of Norwegians hated the invaders and the invasion and provided what support was possible for an active underground resistance. One of the finest of these Norwegians was a man named Claus Helberg, who, with training and support from the western Allies, was able to recruit and lead a team of nine commandos who raided and largely destroyed the Nazi built 'heavy water' plant at Rjuken. The lack of the necessary material from the destroyed Rjuken plant so slowed the Nazi atom bomb research and development that they were not able to resume it before the Allied bombing attacks shut down the rest of their development program. That raid, little noted by the western world at the time, but later celebrated in an American made movie, "The Heroes Of Telemark," was one of the turning points of the war. The nine commandos who completed the raid were able to escape to Sweden and Britain. After the war Helberg became a revered hero in Norway. On his 80th birthday he was honored with a celebratory dinner at which he sat between Queen Sonja of Norway and Queen Margarethe of Denmark. He well deserved the honors he received. Would that the same could have been done for all of my friends and the other 8th Air Force heroes who died in their planes in the performance of their duty.

The other occurance in 1943, seldom mentioned in histories of that war, was the development of a very long range German heavy bomber, the four engine Me-264, which actually took its first flight in late 1942. This plane, called the "Amerika Bomber," could stay in the air for forty five hours and carry two tons of bombs 9500 miles—to America and back, easily. In early 1944 an even more advanced bomber, the six-engine Ju-290, actually flew to New York and took pictures of that city and of Boston, to facilitate a future bombing of those cities and areas. The Germans planned such a bombing campaign against North American cities in early 1944. This action was delayed and then abandoned when the British, with their "Ultra" code breaker providing the ability to read the fabled German 'Enigma' code, months after actually intercepting the information, informed the Americans of the production of the "264" and the "290." The Americans promptly bombed those production facilities and the threat ceased to exist.

This and other tidbits of WW II information are available in a little known book by Dunnigan and Nofi, entitled, "Dirty Little Secrets Of World War II." These gentlemen were also kind enough to share with me, so I could share with you the fact that we in the air saw very little beans, onions, and other gas producing foods in our diet because their well-known gas producing abilities translated to very painful expansion in the intestines during high altitude time in unpressurized airplanes, and planes in WW II were unpressurized. That section of the book is entitled "Farts From Hell", as it well should be.

The "Farts From Hell" no doubt produced a chuckle from you, as it did from me. And it would have when we were flying, although I never heard the phrase, then. We needed chuckles. There was seldom a day that death was not close to us, and a chuckle lightened the tension that fear, the close companion of imminent death, produced in all of us. My first mission was to Munich---9 ½ hour mission. First time I'd ever seen flak. Before, during, and following the bomb run, the sky around us was black with flak. Ninety mm flak is black. Black powder used as the explosive to blow the shell to bits when it reaches our height. One-o-five mm flak is white. Don't know why. The black or white explosive blows the metal shell to a thousand pieces, all of which seem to blow through our ship. Every ship in the Group, that day, was riddled with flak, but no one went down. Can't see why. Most of the shells seem to be 90s. The black powder was so thick that at times we couldn't see our wingmen, but it only lasts a few seconds, then the next burst arrives, then a clear space until the next shell bursts. They arrive in a line, moving toward our wingman, then toward us, then beyond us. We breathe again, until the next bursts arrive, this time in the middle of the formation. We've reached the I.P.—initial point of the bomb run, and turned onto the run. We must fly straight and steady while the bombardier lines up the bomb sight on the target. He's flying the ship, now, with his little control gadget, or he's following the line the lead bombardier is setting, so there's no evasive action allowed. The flak bursts move closer and closer. Then "bombs away" and the entire formation swings to the right, with the outer ships pulling full power, because the swing is just like the game of 'pop-the-whip'. The guys near the end have to move a hell of a lot faster to keep up with the pace setter on the inner end of the line. Our fighters around most of the time, today, so no bandits on us, but they hit some of the other groups pretty hard and the Flak was Hell. On the swing off the bomb run the Group formation was pulled loose and the Group was pulled loose from the Wing. Flak seemed to fill the empty spaces. Heavy, heavy flak and German fighters everywhere, but no one from the 91st went down—a miracle. That was our first mission, on July 12, 1944. The mission was Hell, but miraculously, the 91st had no losses.

"Take-off: 8 a.m. Landing: 5:30. 7 hours on oxygen. Too exhausted to climb out of hatch door below cockpit. Fell out. Kissed the ground, I was so glad to be back on it.

Assembly at 14,000 ft. In at 20,000. Bomb at 25,000. Out at 20,000. Let down from # 7 at 300 degrees. Bomb order: Lead, high, low (sqdn). Flak damage heavy all over Group.

That's a brief of my notes from my first mission.

We flew to the same target the next day—Munich, or Munchen, as it appears on the charts. I say Munich, but we never actually bombed cities or their civilian populations. We were bombing factories producing aircraft, trucks, various kinds of munitions, or military airfields near those cities.

Same flak. We survived again. I kissed the ground again when I fell out of the forward hatch after we stopped engines and filled out the A-1 form. And I'll tell you more about the A-I Form in a bit. For these two missions we had flown an old work-horse of an airplane, Wabash Cannonball. She brought us home, but with so many holes in her that it took ten days to make her flyable again, so we didn't fly again until July 24th, when we flew a different plane. In that interval the Group lost eight planes over Leipzig on July 20th (three from the 322nd) and a few days later, over Halle, on August 16th, lost six more, the whole 324th squadron. We (our crew) were stood down both days. My plane was shot down on Sept. 5th, one of four planes lost in a little more than a week, and then, on a mission to Meresburg on November 2nd, the 91st lost thirteen planes, one of the bloodiest days of the war. How my old crew survived those bloody days, I don't know. The 322 lost nine planes. That's the entire squadron, and a few days before, the 324th had lost everyone. That's not quite true. The ships were lost, true enough, but some of them were replacement ships and crews, just arrived at the group, and a few of the more senior crews survived----including Tom and my crew. In my life of today friends have asked me, "How could you fly, knowing that three out of four planes would not return? I have pondered that and I can only answer that I honesty don't know. Anticipation of disaster and death rode on our shoulders all through our flight time. I remember well, on one of our missions to Ludwigshaven, I happened to have the controls, --we took roughly twenty minute turns at the controls to avoid excessive fatigue—tight formation flying is hard work-----when I heard the rattle of gunfire hitting the body of the plane. I could see no sign of enemy fighters, but I could hear the sound of metal rattling off the skin of the plane. I yelled over the interphone, "Where the hell are we being hit, and why isn't anyone reporting it."

Tom heard me on the interphone; he looked over and nearly fell off his seat with laughter. All of the crew, including the pilots, wore metal helmets on our heads, and flak suits covering much of our bodies. We'd just gone through a terrific burst of flak, and now I thought fighters were hitting us, so I yelled into the mike, "Where are we being hit". Then I saw Tom laughing. He said, "Andy, nothing's hitting us. What you hear is your helmet rattling off the side window as you shake, and I can't tell if it's because you're so scared or so mad." I joined in his laughter, and I never became really frightened, again. Although we were hit with both flak and fighters a number of times so hard that I'm still surprised we survived, the element of visceral fear that I had felt never ruled me again—and the experience stood me in good stead. Years later, when my first job as a principal in an inner city school put me in a position where I came around a corner as a young man came over the fence (to rob some of our students) I was able to say to him, "back over the fence, son." He swung back over the fence, then turned, put a '38 through the fence into my chest, said, "Now I'm going to get you, mother." I was able to say, "No, I don't think you will, son." He hesitated a moment, then put the gun in his pocket, said "I'm not your son, mother," and walked away. I didn't break a sweat. I knew then and I know now that it was the terror of the combat days that made the gun threat seem a minor matter. But that's another book. Now back to those desperate days of war.

While we were on the ground, missing those bloody days in the air when the Group was being decimated, we did more ground school work, refurbished worn skills, and learned from those on the ground with us how lucky we were to be with the 91st, in spite of the current bloodletting. Our crew, crew # 3276, had been put together in Salt Lake City and completed our phase training at Alexandria, Louisiana, in late April of 1944. On May 3, 1944, we were given special order # 124, which sent the 34 crews which had just finished their training at Alexandria on our way to the combat zone, England. We sat on a train for several days on our way to New York, where we boarded an overcrowded freighter for ten days of dodging submarines while we made our way across the Atlantic to England.

But that was more than a year after the first set of missions which I've described, here. For our crew, even on those missions to bomb the factories at Munich where the flak was so heavy that at times we could hardly see past our wingtips, and the German fighters picked at us all of the way in and then out of Europe, Lady Luck had her arm around us. We thought we were hard hit on our first two missions, because the flak nearly tore our plane apart, but the fact that we were so hard hit but still made it back to England literally saved our lives. The damage done to our plane meant that we missed the next few missions, missions on which the 91st was severely damaged. Our first mission, to Munich on July 12,th, was the 91st's 195th mission. They had developed their formation flying skills to a very high level. The gunners had honed their gun skills. The concept of flak vests had been developed and accepted, so that the wounding of crew members, other than as the result of a heavy, direct hit, had diminished appreciably. In Colonel Terry, who was as skilled and capable a leader as could be found anywhere, we had a leader who was highly respected, who could enforce both flying and ground discipline without losing the confidence and respect of his men. In short, by the time our crew and the other crews we trained with, and who were lucky enough to join us at the 91st arrived, the 91st was among the best, if not the very best fighting group of its kind. In spite of that, the combat was so vicious, so deadly, that the loss rate remained near the same until the last days of combat, the end of the war. By that 195th mission the Group had lost 147 B-17s in combat. A number more were lost in training missions, in accidents, etc. but the count made, here, is only of those planes lost in actual combat or in action very close to combat. 147 from a Group strength of 36, where the usual flight strength on a mission was 27, three squadrons of nine planes, each. There were a number of missions on which the full Group strength of 36 planes was flown, but one squadron was usually 'stood down' (rested), so that the usual flight strength was 27. The 91st completed 340 missions, the last being to Pilsen, to hit munitions factories, on April 25, 1945. Mercifully, no ships were lost on that mission, but the total loss in combat, to that time, 207 B-17s, is a staggering number. That is more than 2000 of the most highly skilled fighting men who ever lived. And remember, that is just the loss count from one Group, and there were many Groups, both of B-17s and B-24s, flying, and losing comparable numbers, each day. That's more than 40,000 men from the 8th Air Force, alone, in more than 4,000 heavy bombers, more than 3,000 B-17s and a thousand B-24s.

Some of those men survived the loss of their planes by bailing out and lived in prison camps to the end of the war. Books have been written and movies made of what happened in and in connection with those prisons, but no description can ever be adequate. One of the forced marches of the prisoners, forced by their German captors to avoid the advancing Russians, was the equal of those brutally cruel marches made by American prisoners in the Phillipines, with lagging prisoners being tortured and shot by the accompanying German guards. Americans should never forget what that generation of young men endured, suffered through, and accomplished in the service of their country and their comrades. As Tom Brokaw said in his book, "The Greatest Generation" it was indeed that, the "Greatest Generation". Never in human history, with the exception, perhaps, of those who fought and died at Thermopalae, was there a group or a sacrifice like it. Now on to that story.

That loss of 147 planes up to the time when my crew began to fly was four times the full strength of the Group. Other groups had similar loss rates, but the 91st flew more missions, lost more aircraft and crews, and received more awards and decorations than any other group in the war. No other group will ever match it. As you have read, the day I was shot down I was riding as an experienced pilot with a new crew. That was part of the usual routine for new crews.

They were given all of the training and help which could be given, but still the greatest loss rate was constantly among crews which were relatively new to the group. My own crew, the TomGordon/Andy Anderson crew, was one of the few which flew a full count of missions and returned home as a group (without me) when that count was complete. Our crew, crew #3276 in training and on the way to combat, and renumbered at Bassingbourn as crew #H-67, was a re-assignment, or 'filler' crew, sent to Bassingbourn when we arrived at a reassignment station in England to replace one of the 36 planes and crews which had been lost in the four short months before we arrived. That was the equivalent of the entire group, and, as we learned, years later, other group's losses were similar, or greater. Those numbers were not published or discussed while we were there, for morale reasons, but we all knew, unofficially, what the loss rate was. Oddly, the highest loss rate was among the newest crews. None of us knew why, or if there was a reason, but quite a few of the crews who began together finished together, while the newer crew faces simply disappeared. The fate of the crew I flew with that day was and is a good example, and I can't tell you why. As far as I could tell, we did everything right that day, but a piece of steel from a flak shell got us and slowed us up enough that we became a sitting duck, and we went down. As you have read, the 91st lost 206 other B-17s. I'll quote a report from Sam Halpert, of the 324th, our sister squadron, a little later in this account, telling of the heroic actions of two crews who were able to survive and return from a mission to Munich. Those ships came back, as did many others with similar damage, but remember, there were 207 planes that did not. They were blown apart in the air, or so damaged that their crews were forced to bail out, to become prisoners of war. We will never know the stories of what happened to them, of the heroic battles they fought, and of their desperate, ultimate destruction. The stories you will read from Sam, from me, and from a few others, are of those who survived, but remember, 207 B-17s, from our Group alone, did not. And we were only one of the dozens of Heavy Bomber Groups who flew out of that vast airbase, England, for those long, desperate months of bloody warfare. We flew those magnificent airships, the B-17s, through missions of almost unimaginable stress. Those few of us who survived knew how lucky we were, but we flew again the next day, or the next week, knowing that two out of three of us would never come back.

And it was not a matter of care, of maintenance. We had heroic ground crews, who kept all of our ships in the best condition possible. They did a great job. Whenever we flew a ship the first thing the pilots, and the rest of the crew did, in their own areas, was to preflight the ship. That means that each of us went through a lengthy check list—a list so long that we didn't rely on memory. That list is kept (was, and is, today, in today's planes) at each crew member's station. The list is for the part of the plane and equipment that that crew member is responsible for, and woe betide any crew member who does not complete his check list. If a gunner neglects to check something on his gun(s) and it later fails in the air, the whole crew may die. If a pilot neglects to check an instrument, or a tire, etc. and it later fails, the whole crew may die. Any failure or shortcoming on the plane is reported to the pilot, who writes it on the A-1 form before he leaves the plane, and the first thing he does when he is seated in the cockpit is to check the A-1 form, to see that any problem that existed has been corrected before the plane flies again. And airplanes are such intricate, complicated machines that problems, some of them correctable and some of them not, always exist. All maintenance problems are listed on the A-1 form, but maintenance crews do have a sense of humor. George Birdsong, in his book, "Stormy Weather, A B-17," (one of the best books ever written about World War II and the B-17's part in it) listed some of the problems and their solutions that were written up in B-17 A-1 forms. I'll list them here, too.

Problem: Left inside main tire almost needs replacement.
Solution: Almost replaced left inside main tire.
Problem: Test flight OK, except auto land very rough.
Solution: Autoland not installed on this aircraft.
Problem # 1: #2 propeller seeping prop fluid.
Solution # 1: #2 propeller seepage normal.
Problem # 2: #1, #3, and # 4 propellers lack normal seepage.
Problem: The autopilot doesn't.
Solution: It does, now.

Problem: Something loose in cockpit.
Solution: Something tightened in cockpit.
Problem: Evidence of hydraulic leak on right main gear.
Solution: Evidence removed.
Problem: Number three engine missing.
Solution: Engine found on right wing after brief search.
Problem: Pilot's relief tube too short.
Solution: Pilot's relief tube long enough. Pilot's equipment too short.

One of my friends, Mike Banta, whom I met years after the war via the 91st computer site, has written a book entitled "Vignettes of a B-17 Crew. He said I could quote from it if I gave him credit, so I am doing that, now. It's a well-written record of the missions that he and his crew flew. He publishes it himself. You can buy it from him by contacting him at his computer address, which is B17Banta@aol.com The book is fascinating. I'll share two stories from it with you, one of which, "The Relief Tube", I'm very familiar. The other, the "Chicken" story is one I wish someone on my crew had thought of while we were flying. The "Relief Tube" problem is one which every air crew meets in its own way, but no one ever found a satisfactory solution.

There were no toilets on warplanes in WW II, but human bodies need urine and bowel relief. Crew members bring along buckets for that purpose, use them, and dump them at the end of a mission. All crew members, except the pilots, can move around the ship during a mission, but the pilots, because of the exigencies of flight, or of combat, often are unable to leave their seats. Bowels can often be habit trained, but kidneys are not so trainable, so there are times when a bladder must be emptied, and at twenty five thousand feet and sixty to seventy degrees below zero, which was often the case when we flew, a flying suit soaked with urine is so intolerable that it may mean tragedy for the airplane, which MUST be under complete pilot control at all times. To solve, or partially solve, this problem, a relief tube, a four inch funnel, is placed in a clamp between and beneath the two pilots. The funnel is attached to a tube which is vented out the bottom of the plane. When the need arises, (and only when it's pretty desperate) the pilot in need reaches down, unclips the funnel and pulls it up to where he can urinate into it---IF he can get the front of his flying suit and/or other clothing unfastened so that he can urinate into the tube, while keeping one hand on the control wheel in front of him. It worked. Not well, but it worked---IF the tube where it

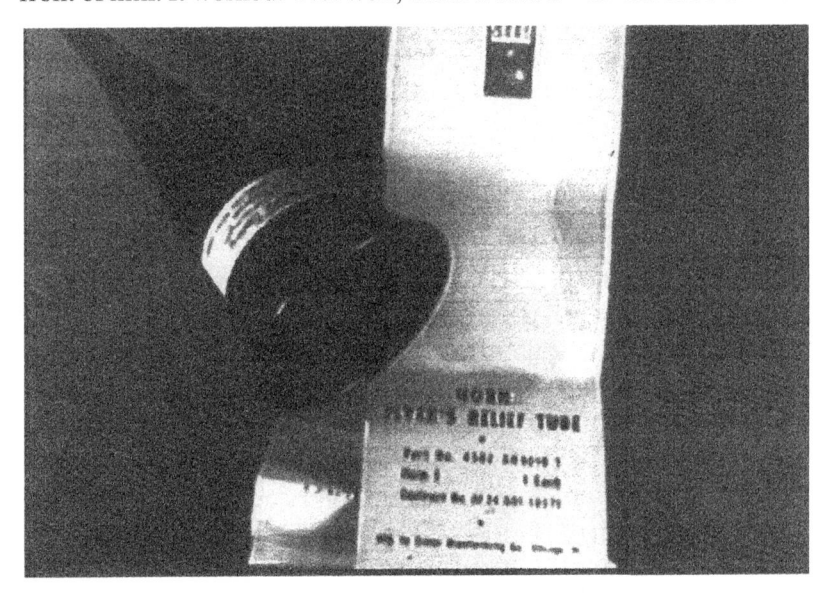

The Horn of the Flyer's Relief Tube
This instrument assisted the airmen with bathroom
breaks while on combat missions.

exited the plane didn't freeze from the moisture it was carrying, IF there wasn't a kink in the hose, and several other ifs. The catch in all of this is that the tube vented outside the ship just in front of the ball turret, where the ball turret gunner was doing his best to exist and to keep the pilots informed if an enemy approached. It was the pilot's duty to inform the ball turret gunner when he was about to use the relief tube, so that the turret gunner could turn the turret so the yellow liquid splashing on the turret and freezing immediately, splashed on the backside of the turret, not the front. The exit line often froze, the line would fill up, and the pilot would be left to decide what to do next. It never happened to me, but Mike tells of the time when it happened to him. He was left with his bladder half emptied, the relief line full and frozen shut and no help in sight. He solved the situation that time by reaching for his flak helmet, which was sitting at his feet, finishing emptying his bladder into the helmet, and hoping a violent movement of the ship did not tip the helmet before the mission was completed. It sounds funny as hell, now, but it wasn't funny for us at the time, and I wouldn't be surprised if more than one disaster had a connection to this problem. Mike also tells of the time when he reached for the relief tube to pull it up to where he needed it. It had had a piece cut out of the tubing. He never found out why, but he was able to release his safety belt, climb out of his cockpit seat, move partway down the steps into the nose and relieve himself, then put the funnel back into its clip, climb back into the cockpit and resume flying. After landing, as is required after every flight, he wrote up the problem on the A-1 form, saying, "The hose is too short to use." The next time he climbed into the cockpit he picked up the A-1 form to check that the plane had been readied for flight. It is required that whatever had been written up by the previous pilot be corrected and noted in the A-1 for whoever flies the plane next. This time it was Mike. A check had been put beside his previous note, and another note added in the "Corrections made" section, saying "Plane's equipment all right. Pilot's equipment too short." (But a length HAD been added to the hose, so it was now usable). Mike also tells of the time when, on the way home from a long mission, six hours in the air up to then, his navigator stuck his head up from his position in the nose section and asked, "You hungry?" They were always hungry. Breakfast had been more than nine hours earlier. They'd eaten the few candy bars they carried for just this situation hours ago, and hunger pangs were consuming them. The navigator, Johnny, asked, "You like a piece of hot chicken?" Mike said, knowing that he was kidding, "I'd love one." In a moment Johnny reappeared with a piece of hot chicken for Mike, one for Ray, the co-pilot, and one for George, the flight engineer standing behind them. "How in the world did you perform this miracle?" Mike asked. Johnny answered that he had gone to the messhall before breakfast, talked the cook out of as many pieces of fried chicken as he could carry, wrapped them in waxed paper, carried them aboard, and when they were on their way home, he'd put them into one of the electrically heated gloves that we wore at altitude. Voila!! Hot fried chicken. Johnny had beaten the airlines by at least a decade in providing hot food during flight.

Now let me tell you a little more about the group of missions I've been describing. I'm up to the 22nd mission, which was a deciding mission in the course of the war. By the time that mission was completed the Group had lost sixteen of its planes and crews in combat. With the two or three which had been lost through accident or malfunction (and thus not counted as combat losses, though the crews were just as dead). That was half of our group. Other groups had similar or higher losses. That meant that half of our available combat force had been destroyed in a combat period of four months. Was it worth it?

On March 4, a valiant 22 year old major, Paul Fishburne, led a mission which, in part, determined not only the future course, but the eventual outcome of the war. The heavy bomber losses had been such that it was problematical that the losses we were able to inflict on the German war machine were worth the losses we were undergoing. We had bombed docks, airfields and railroad yards, largely in France, but the Allies had not yet been able to reach deep into Germany to slow the war materiel production which was supporting the German war effort. The 91st mission of March 4th, led by the audacious young major Fishburne, put a different face on the accomplishments of the bombing force and the effect they were having and would have on the eventual outcome of the war. Fishburne, as noted in Bert Humphries' account near the beginning of this record, was the commander of the 322nd squadron of the 91st. It was highly unusual, even in those days, for a 22 year old to bear the rank of major, but Fishburne had earned it. The 91st had flown 21 missions to that date, and Fishburne had been a part of most of them. In those 21 missions the group had already lost twelve ships, nearly half of the usual group strength of 27. The fighting had been fierce, but the learning curve had mounted steeply. Formation skills had been developed to a high level, gunners had honed their own skills, and all of the crews, in spite of the fact that the group had flown only 21 missions, felt that they were seasoned veterans. To them 21 missions was a lifetime. None of the crews had been on all 21 of those missions, but most of the crews had been on a majority of them. Remember, the

Group had only been flying for four months. The first mission was to the submarine docks at Brest on November 4th. The first aircraft lost, beside the 401st plane lost on the flight over, were the three lost on the November 21 mission to the sub pens at St. Nazaire. Those were Pandora's Box, and DF (no name) of the 324th squadron., and Sad Sack, of the 323rd. Since then they had lost two planes, LL (no name), and LL-E, Danellen, of the 401st, on a mission to hit a fighter field at Romilly-sur-Seine, in France, another on a mission to hit the U-boat pens at Lorient on Dec. 30th, (Short Snorter), and our eighth loss, Panhandle Dogey, on a mission to hit the sub pens at St. Nazaire on January 3rd, the first mission of what was to be a heart-breaking group of losses in the new year, 1943. On that mission to St. Nazaire the B-17s of the 91st put into effect a new combat flight doctrine—tight formation flying. It was a new skill, developed as the need arose. With the loss of Panhandle Dogey we had lost nearly a third of our usual flight group of 27 planes, and more than 240 highly skilled combat crewmen. At that rate, in another three months the whole group would be gone. Intolerable. And though no crewman ever refused to fly, morale was dropping to a new low. Now, from where we never knew, came a saving grace, a new combat design. Each B-17 carried ten-sometimes more, sometimes fewer, but usually ten—fifty caliber machine guns, but their effectiveness was limited by their placement. If a fighter approached from the side, only three of the 50s could fire at him. That was formidable. Each 50 calibre shell weighed half a pound, and was deadly, if it hit what it was aimed at, but the planes cruised at about 150 miles per hour, the air was usually rough, and the temperature at 20,000 feet or more was 60 to 70 degrees below zero. Bare fingers which touched the guns at those temperatures froze to them. The surgeons developed new techniques to remove frozen fingers from hands and many gunners flew with fewer fingers than they began with, but those were comparatively minor complaints. Death rode on the shells of the attacking fighters. The skills of their pilots had been learned on the Russian front, where some of the German pilots had more than 200 combat kills. The new combat design was a formation which placed a wingman on each side of the squadron leader and a fourth below and behind and had three of those elements of four planes in a squadron fly as a unit, with a lead squadron, a high squadron, and a low squadron. That group of 27 was a normal group strength, but it varied, depending on the needs of the day, the number of planes flyable at the time, or the size of the bombing force required. That formation aimed from 108 to 216 fifty caliber machine guns at approaching fighter planes, focusing heavy destructive firepower on those fighters. Flying tight formation requires tremendous skill, with constant throttle adjustments and control movements to keep the formation in shape and tight. The new formation shape was put into effect by the 91st on that 8th mission, to St. Nazaire, and was adopted throughout the 8th Air Force as its benefits became apparent. The crews flying then had to learn on the job, but those of us who came later learned in our months in training before we were sent to combat zones. The formations provided a great deal of protection from German fighters, but they made the Groups more vulnerable to the German flak, ground fire, because the individual planes had to hold position in the formation. No individual evasive action could be taken, so I remember, vividly, watching the flak bursts off our wing move in closer to us as the ground gunners locked onto our altitude and speed, until the next flak burst would be in our ship or past us. Fortunately, during my limited (15 missions) tour, the flak seldom centered on us enough to demolish us, although there were several times when I was sure it would. The 91st was first in many things. In the early months so many men were being killed or badly wounded by flak, which is simply a heavy (90 mm or 105mm) shell shot up to our altitude, then exploded so that the pieces of the shell casing pierce anything within the radius of the shell explosion—so many crew members were being wounded and thus incapacitated, that something had to be done to lessen the damage. Some bright soul had the idea of a solid mesh of canvas covered steel rings, made into a half-body length type of apron, worn over both the front and the back, covering the body from the waist up. They were heavy, but their use immediately and precipitously decreased the damage done to the bodies of the crew members. The 91st was selected to try out the new flak suits. Because of the heavy body damage we'd been suffering, their value was so clear to crew members that it was not long before an order came down from on high that crew members were not to so surround themselves with flak suits that the plane was overloaded and difficult to fly. The principal purpose of the plane was to carry bombs, not flak suits. This order was honored in absentia. Flak suits were often so scattered through the plane that the pilot would have to order the crew to throw some of them out before the plane took off.

    It was never said as such to us, but it was not too long before the principal purpose of the heavily armed B-17s became to destroy enemy fighters, so that as the bombing proceeded, the German fighting armada was gradually destroyed, and the bombing attacks upon the German war materiel production facilities became successful enough so that the Germans would gradually run out of war supplies, and thus be unable to repel the Allied invasion forces when the inevitable invasion occurred. This theory, and its eventual implementation, was proved correct, but for many months, years, really, it was touch and go. By the time I was shot down, in September of 1944, there were few German men left in Germany. Most German men were in the army. Those that were left to work in the production plants, both for war materiel and home use, were simply not enough to do the job, so much of the German production in the last years of the war was done by slave labor, the labor of prisoners who had been captured during the early years of the war, and now were used as slave labor to replace the German men who were serving in the armed forces. My Russian comrades were two of these captured soldier/slaves. There were thousands more like them throughout the German homeland. The Russians looked with strong disfavor on soldiers who allowed themselves to be captured rather than be killed by the Germans. Years later, when I tried to find our friends, Paul and Tim-o-fey, they were nowhere to be found. The French priest in Baslieuse made known to the Russians, when they arrived deep into Germany, that there were two Russian soldiers in Alsace-Lorraine. The Russians sent soldiers to get them, and they did, ignoring our friends' fervent requests that they be allowed to remain with the French people who had fed and hidden them for so long. Paul and Tim-o-fey were taken back to Russia, and quite probably ended their lives at hard labor in a Siberian labor camp. I will always regret leaving them, although they quite probably would have refused to come with us if we had asked them. The villagers would not answer my questions about what happened to the priest, but I got the impression that he did not long survive the end of the fighting.

Years later, after I had acquired something of a reputation as an educator, I had an opportunity to be a part of a small group of educators who were to go to the USSR (Moscow) to share some of our experience and insights in the education and treatment of problem youths. Seven of us were chosen as a representative group of knowledgeable people who might be helpful to the Russian education establishment. Hosted by the Russian Government, we flew to Moscow and met with the Russian Minister of Education and members of his staff. Our first meeting was for dinner in the Kremlin. The minister asked what our purpose was in being there. Somewhat puzzled, we answered that we were there to give what help we could in developing ways to handle the education of youths with exceptional problems. The minister said, "We don't have any problems here that we need help with." Then he stood and walked out. One of his assistants, who stayed and talked with us, said, in effect, "The hell we don't." We were housed in luxury quarters where notables were ordinarily housed, and fed the same way, but the Yeltsin revolution was in progress, and sure enough, as one of the minister's assistants had intimated to us the evening before, the next day the education bureaucracy underwent a complete change, and our mission deteriorated into a ten day series of visits to schools and conferences with minor officials. Because our American group leader had been in Moscow several times, she knew a number of people there, and we were invited to a few homes to visit with the people. Homes in Moscow are not homes in the sense that we know them in the United States. Homes are small apartments, or flats, in the innumerable twenty to thirty story apartment buildings which fill the city, and most of which, as far as we could see, were dangerously deteriorated and in need of repair. Each time we used an elevator to ascend to whatever floor we were visiting, we held our collective breaths for fear the elevator would cease operating in the midst of our ascent. And few of those elevators held more than four people. Food, when we shared a meal with the occupants, consisted largely of potatoes, in one form or another, usually flavored with some cheese. Liquor, however, never seemed to be in short supply and was consumed in a quantity which was unbelievable to us. One of the other principals in our group was from Montana, and he also was a Mormon, so the two of us were usually able to convince our Russian friends that we had a religious prohibition against consuming strong drink, although I don't believe they ever really believed us. We were always offered vodka and/or wines when we visited families, but we usually ate at our hotel (a luxury hotel used, prior to the Yeltsin revolution, to host visiting dignitaries, on the order of kings or presidents) or in the Kremlin, itself, and in the hotel or the Kremlin we were always under pressure to drink on the same level (and quantity) as our hosts, which was simply not possible for us, because most of us drank moderately, and the man from Montana and me, not at all, but our glasses were always kept filled, so we learned a lot about drinking (and how to politely avoid it) and some of us acquired some new tastes. But it was fun. I say fun, but that word never occurred to any of us, then. Life in Moscow, especially at that time, is deadly serious, and we were pressed as to how to accomplish our mission, especially as the Russians had paid for most of it. It was a problem for me, because my principal motive in getting to Moscow was to see if I could find any trace of my friends, Paul and Tim-o-fey. Unhappily, there was no way. The government offices were so disorganized, at that moment, that I found that there was no one in the whole city who could, or would, help me in my quest. And now that I look back on it, I really don't believe any record was kept of our two friends after the Russian troops picked them up at Baslieuse. Well, I had a good look at schools in Moscow (schools and kids are much the same anywhere) and my heart still aches that I never saw or heard of Paul or Tim-o-fey again after we left them in the cave. Tim-o-fey saved my life more than once---sometimes with his knife and sometimes with his uncanny ability to anticipate German patrols and actions. Enough of that. I couldn't find any trace of them in Moscow, but I retain a vivid memory of the snow laden branches of the trees which line the runway of the airport near Moscow, where we landed, of the schools in Moscow with their crumbling concrete, even though, in most cases, they were relatively new, and of the delightful children in those schools.

Now back to that incredible mission to Hamm, led by Major Fishburne. Fishburne was one of the four original squadron commanders as the Group came overseas. He commanded the 322nd through the Group's first 21 missions. The mission to Hamm was its 22nd. The other squadron commanders, as the Group arrived in England and began its missions, were: 323rd, Major Paul Brown, 324th, Major Haley Aycock, and 401st, Captain Clyde Gillespie.

The 91st had flown two missions in the previous week---to the docks at Wilhelmshaven on February 26th, and to the sub pens at Brest on the 27th. Both were strenuous missions. Short Snorter II and Kickapoo were lost on the 26th, and though there were no losses, the mission to Brest on the 27th was a difficult one, with considerable damage to several planes. As a result, only 20 planes were available for the mission to Hamm on March 4, and four of those planes aborted early in the mission due to mechanical problems. Briefing was at 6 a.m. When the cover was raised, at briefing, and the long red line leading to Hamm, in the Ruhr Valley, the first mission that deep into the heart of the German homeland, was revealed, silence reigned in the briefing room. Then murmers arose as notes were taken as to rendezvous, routing, flare codes, etc. Chutes were picked up, briefing groups were loaded to be transported to plane bays, where bombs had been placed, guns and ammunition delivered and crew members checked and rechecked their responsibilities. Pilots and co-pilots completed an external pre-flight of their planes, then swung aboard through the nose hatch to do the internal pre-flight check. And that pre-flight check was vital. There were literally hundreds of checks which must be made before take-off. Preparation for the extreme cold soon to be experienced demanded careful preparation. I have seen the external temperature gauge on the dashboard of the cockpit register a minus seventy degrees on many occasions. And that was not a short-term measurement. We flew at that temperature for hours, wearing oxygen masks where the steam from our breathing froze into blocks of ice that then had to be broken out while we checked each other to be sure we did not pass out from lack of oxygen during our short time without the mask on our faces. With one exception there was no heat for the crew in the body of that four engine machine gunned fortress, the B-17. That exception was the flight deck, essentially the cockpit, where glycerin which had been heated in a boiler in the nacelle of one of the engines heated air which was then pumped through air ducts onto the flight deck. Some of the heated air was blown against the windshield and side windows of the cockpit so that those areas did not ice or fog up and leave the pilots blind. The heat was controlled by a lever under the left window adjacent to the pilot, so when the heating system was working, the pilot and co-pilot's fingers and toes were usable. When any part of the heat stream failed, or was shot out, as on our mission on August 30th, to Kiel, it became so bitterly cold in the cockpit, as it always was in the rest of the airplane, that normal physical action was almost impossible. The machine guns throughout the ship became so cold that to touch one without gloves meant instant frostbitten fingers. Nevertheless, in the intensity of combat, when a gun jammed, as they often did, and because working with gloves on was difficult and frustrating, often a gunner would try to undo a jam with bare fingers. Mike Banta, in his book, "Vignettes Of A Combat Crew" says that the frostbitten fingers that resulted occurred so often that the flight surgeons (back on the ground) developed a routine procedure for treatment. They would not surgically remover the damaged finger, but they would allow the finger to die back to a live joint. The finger would turn black and wither up to that point, and then fall off, leaving the stump. With this method of sterilization infection would not set in, and the stub, with the balance of the finger, would survive and soon be back in service. Mike recounts also, which I can confirm, that our exhaling breath, through our oxygen masks, carried an infinitesimal amount of moisture, and, instead of dissipating, at times that moisture would turn into a snowflake, and, because its enlarged surface made it lighter than air, it would float upward. So we would have an upward falling snowstorm, and, eventually, a snow carpeted roof in the cockpit. And those older B-17 models did not have hydraulic controls, as the later models did. We flew those babies with muscle power. It was hard work, and we sweated a lot—but it was so cold that the sweat froze immediately. Our faces were often covered with beads of ice. On a long, high mission we all became "Frosty, the Snowman." And we all, well practically all, learned to pretty much control our bodily functions. You've heard already that there were no toilets on B-17s. Try sitting on the rim of an icy bucket when what comes out freezes almost as soon as it exits. And that problem almost killed us, once. Our crew was put together in Salt Lake City. None of us knew any of the rest of the crew. We got acquainted on the long train ride to Alexandria, La., where we were sent for B-17 combat crew training. Tom, the 1st pilot, had already gone through preliminary B-17 training, so he know how to fly one of the big ships, but I, the new co-pilot, just out of flight school, had never been near one. So I learned as we went, and fortunately, none of our crew knew how much I didn't know, and neither did Tom. With the ego of a twenty year old, eager to show how much I knew, I was reluctant to ask for help (which my wife of more then fifty years says is still one of my problems). Right at the beginning of our B-17 training we began to learn formation flying, which takes a high degree of skill and instantaneous hand/arm/foot coordination. On the first, or one of the first days of our training, we eased into a formation for the first time—and pretty close, almost wing-tip to wing-tip. Just as we eased into position, Tom had a bowel urge. He released his safety belt, said, "You got it, Andy," and went back into the radio room to use the bucket. We hadn't done ANY formation flying in advanced training. In my Advanced school, at Blythville, Arkansas, we'd learned multi-engine flying in an odd little twin engine trainer called an AT (advanced trainer) 9. it was a good little ship, but the transition from my single-engine Basic, (intermediate) school BT (Basic Trainer) 13, to the twin engine AT-9, which was kind of "hot"—meaning that it landed at a fairly high speed and needed a good deal of practice to handle properly, took so much time that there wasn't enough time to do any formation training, so we simply didn't get any, and worst of all, we didn't know how much we didn't know. We were the cream of young America. We had survived the intense weeding-out of Pre-flight, and the follow-up weeding-out of Primary training, where we actually learned to fly. More than half of us had been siphoned off in the intense selection processing at Pre-flight. Another twenty-five percent, who just weren't suited for the high pressure intensity of actually learning to fly and the mass of learning and physical conditioning which went with it, were drained off in Basic and Advanced flight training schools, so that by the time we received our wings and those gold Second Lieutenant's bars at 'Advanced' graduation, we thought we knew everything. How wrong we were. And how little we knew. I hadn't had any practice in the constant throttle changes and aileron and rudder adjustments which had to be made to stay in formation, so our plane drifted back and forth in the sky, with me trying to make throttle and control adjustments to keep in formation. It was like jumping off a high diving board without knowing how to swim or to dive, except that in a dive you only hit the water with a splash, but in the air, if the wings hit, they crumpled and you died. Tom came running back with his pants half down, yelling, "Andy, keep it steady." We survived. Tom taught me what I needed to know, and I remember, vividly, on the return from a long mission, when Nazi fighters were lurking on the edges of our formation, flying with my wing so close to the wingtip of our wingman that he shook his fist at me. One extra gust of turbulence and our wingtips would have collided and we would both have gone down. But our long training paid off. We didn't collide. The enemy fighters kept their distance, and we made it home again.

From my graduation in class 44A (that means the class of January, 1944) I, like all of the other graduates, was given a ten day leave to visit my family in Utah, near Salt Lake City. I grew up in Utah, in a little town named Mt. Pleasant, right in the center of Utah. The fifteen years I spent there were very happy years, but for various reasons I finished my high school at Polytechnic High School, in the center of Los Angeles, just a few blocks from USC, the University of Southern California, where I later did much of my graduate work, but that was much later. I lucked out in landing at Poly. It was an excellent school, but with its more than two thousand students it was so much bigger than the tiny school in Mt. Pleasant where I began high school that it took a good deal of learning before I learned which way to move through the crowded halls of Poly. And once I learned, I didn't want to leave. My family was in Los Angeles because an uncle, who was a physician there, had called my mother to say to her that her oldest son, Don, (my brother) who had somehow wrangled his way into dental school at USC, was dying of pneumonia, and we had better come down there for the funeral. I say "somehow" because we never did know how he did it, but somehow, after completing two years at Brigham Young University in Utah, Don got word that he had been admitted to the dental school at USC. It was 1939, the depth of the depression years. our father was a country school teacher, who, because Utah did not pay teachers enough to do more than barely survive, had also been a stockman, raising sheep on land in the beautiful Wasatch Mountain foothills, on the land which he, my grandfather, and my aunt had homesteaded in the mountains beyond those foothills. I spent my summers as a little boy, helping, (probably interfering is a better description,) my father run (meaning supervising their grazing) one herd of sheep, while Don ran a second herd a couple of miles away. The fishing, in a mountain stream filled with beaver dams, was great. I had a horse of my own long before I was big enough to climb on by myself. I spent innumerable hours carving my name into the soft white bark of the beautiful Quaken Asp trees which filled the mountains. Life was idyllic. Then came the great crash of 1929. My father and grandfather, who had borrowed money to expand their sheepherds, struggled on for a few years, then lost their sheep and their land to the bank, which had been so willing to finance them when times were good. Times became very hard. Most people in our little town raised much of their food in vegetable gardens. Potatos and carrots were buried in sand so they would not spoil during the long Utah winter. Mothers canned and bottled fruit and vegetables. Every family had a cow, which grazed the pasture which was a part of the yard where the house stood. Mornings and evenings, as soon as I was big enough, I milked that cow, poured the milk into large but shallow round pans, carried the pans into the underground storage cellar where they stood while the heavy cream rose to the top. The next day the pans were brought up, the cream skimmed off and churned into butter. Mormons didn't drink coffee, so the usual table drink was cold milk, with fresh, hot bread and thick butter. My mouth still waters as I remember.

Ah, I have wandered from the story of that historic mission flown by the 91st on March 4, 1943. That mission may have had a part in changing the progress of the war and the history of our civilization.. At least it had a large part in determining the future of the bombing missions of the 91st, and of the entire 8th Air Force, but since I have wandered, let me wander a little further before I come back to the 91st, and the war. You have read that I grew up in Utah, but that I graduated from high school in Los Angeles, then was drafted and sent to a swarming draftee camp near San Bernardino, not far from Los Angeles. I had never seen an army or any other service officer, so when I saw the many officers in the camp, doing nothing much, I thought, but walk around in those beautiful pink, (really steel gray, but they were called 'pinks') or dark green uniforms, I thought that would be a pretty good way to spend my army time. There was a lot for me to learn, however. At first I thought the constant drilling, at which we spent countless hours, was fun, but it soon lost its charm, so when I walked down a camp street, one day, and saw a sign, "Cadet sign ups," I walked up the pathway to the tent with the sign and said, "What's that?" The sergeant at the table said, "You'd like to learn to fly, son?" I said, "Sure." He said, "Sign here." I did and entered the Army Air Corps (as it was called then) Cadet program and a new life. After high school, while waiting to be drafted, I'd worked for a semester on the night shift at the Douglas Aircraft plant in Santa Monica, while attending USC in the daytime on a music scholarship, but I'd never been near an airplane, so it was all new to me. My job at Douglas had been cutting pieces of various metals to be used elsewhere in the plant in the actual manufacture of airplanes, but I'd never been close to one of the flying machines, so I looked forward to the experience when the sergeant told me that "Cadets" meant that I could actually learn to fly.

Those of us who were curious enough to sign up for the "Cadet" experience were put through a few days of tests to weed out those who weren't bright enough to make it through the "Cadet" program, then we were put on a train and sent to Montgomery, Alabama---long train ride, sitting up, no bunks on those trains—to what was called "Preflight School" in Montgomery. There we were put through a thorough testing program. First, to see if we had the intellectual capacity to absorb the intensive training we would undergo if we entered the "Cadet" program, and then to see if we had the mental toughness and physical stamina to make it through the year of speeded up training necessary to become army (later Air Force) officers of one kind or another. The principal aim was to see what type of training we were best suited for. All of us, of course, wanted to become pilots, but two thirds of us were directed into programs which would train us to become navigators or bombardiers. I was one of the fortunate ones who were told that we did well enough in the testing so that we could have our choice of training programs. I chose pilot, of course. About half of the guys who had come east on the train with us didn't make it through the testing and were sent back to the infantry or other training. I knew some of the men who didn't make it through were more able than I, so I felt lucky to be kept in the program.

The only way they had of judging us was how we did on the testing they put us through, and our physical conditioning. I guess I did pretty well on the testing and I'd been a runner in high school, after the years of chasing my father's sheep up and down the mountains sides in Utah, so I was in good enough physical shape. The program was run on the same general plan as the service schools, with our underclass training lasting a little more than a month, and our upperclass training a little more than another month, during which time we absorbed the rough equivalent of a year of college training in mathematics, meteorology, cartography, military skills, small weapons training, physical training and conditioning, etc. The hazing from the upper class got a little rough, sometimes. We lived through it, but I developed a lifelong distaste for that kind of training and have never approved of it. We had the same general code of behavior as the cadets at West Point and Annapolis. When asked, at line-up in the morning, by an upper classman, if I had shaved that day, I was always able to answer, "Yes," truthfully, even though the razor I used often didn't have a blade in it because the fuzz on my face was not yet firm enough to respond to a razor.

When the captain (a real captain, not a cadet) in charge of our unit, (I had been made a cadet lieutenant in charge of a barracks) called me in one day and told me he was giving me a special assignment, I held my breath. We never knew what odd tasks we were going to be given, but all he said was that his sister was arriving for the upcoming dance. College girls from Nashville had been invited to a dance to provide some social life for us, and the captain said I was to be his sister's date so he could keep an eye on her. Then he looked at my shoes and asked if I had any others. We had all been issued G.I. clothes, which included infantry boots. Some of the guys had been able to locate dress shoes, but I hadn't dreamed I'd have any use for them, so I hadn't bought any. I said, "No sir," so he sighed and said his sister would have to live through it. As a cadet lieutenant I'd been issued a saber to wear on ceremonial occasions. I didn't have any idea how ceremonial this occasion was, so I wore the saber, with my G.I. shoes and white gloves, which constituted my dress uniform, to the dance. I don't remember what I did with the saber while we danced. I don't believe it would have enhanced my minuscule dancing skills, but we did enjoy the dance. She was a nice, and very attractive, young lady. She came back to see me a time or two before I moved on to flight school, but in the later ferocity of war, we lost touch. I regretted it.

On the train coming east to Montgomery the dozen of us from Los Angeles became acquainted. I'd graduated from Polytech, in Los Angeles, a comprehensive high school not far from U.S.C. "Comprehensive," in Los Angeles, meant that the school included a number of educational tracks: college prep, industrial arts, music, commercial, business, etc. Poly was an excellent school. Large, with a student body of near 3,000, which made it both advantageous and disadvantageous for me. Excellent traditions, both in academics and artistic and other areas, and athletics, which interested me. They still had a picture of Tom Bradley on the wall in the athletic office. Tom, later the four-term Los Angeles mayor and California near-governor, had been a hurdler of such ability six years before that they still talked about him. I'll come back and talk about that later, though, because knowing Tom colors what I'm going to tell you, later, about my life in the inner city after the war years, but now back to flight schools, and then to combat and that vital mission led by Major Fishburne. First, though, I left us on the train to Montgomery. Those few of us from Los Angeles got to know each other. I became friends with one who'd gone to Hollywood High, while I attended Poly, Flem Astrup. Flew could do almost anything mechanical, an area in which I did not shine, and he was willing to help me in those areas where I needed it, and I needed it a lot, so we became friends and roomed together through most of our flight school training. Roomed together is too strong a word, however. I don't think we ever had an actual room, but we usually had side by side bunks and helped each other when the need arose. In my case it was when we were studying engines or similar problems. I don't know how I helped him, but I must have because we remained friends. There was one real difference, though. I looked for girls. Flem didn't. He had such a case on a girl he'd known at Hollywood High that he brought her out when we were in Basic flight school. And I could see why. She was very, very pretty, and just as nice. They married and he lived part time off the base, which wasn't enough for them, but they made do---so I now had a part time bunkmate. None of us realized it at the time, but life must have been very hard for those women who accompanied their husbands through flight training. We were seldom in one place long enough for them to hold a job. Money, for them, was always short, friendships were made and dissolved every month as we progressed in our flying skills and moved from school to school. Somehow Flem and I stayed on the same track. When we were about to graduate from Primary, in Jackson, we both came down with an unexplained fever and were in the hospital for ten days, so our graduation was delayed and we moved from class 43 K to class 44 A. All of our friends moved one class ahead of us, but we had the advantage of gaining more hours in the air to polish our rudimentary flying skills. Jackson, Mississippi, was desperately hot in the summer. Air conditioning was unknown and our sheets were always soaked with perspiration by morning. Our daily five mile runs and our hours of free-style basketball in the evening, until it became too dark to play, put us into such razor-edge physical shape that we welcomed most of the challenges that we faced, and constant challenges there were, physical and mental.

But first, a little bit about how we got there. Flem grew up in Los Angeles, but I was there by accident. I grew up, and my character was formed, to the extent that it could be formed, in Utah. I say "to the extent that it could be formed" because I believe that so long as we live we never cease to change, to grow. I am not the same person today that I was yesterday because of what I have learned in the intervening time, and I will be a different person tomorrow. At least I hope I never cease learning, and never cease growing. Andrew

Carnegie had a great deal to do with my growing, bless him. He donated money to build libraries all over America. One of them was built in Mt. Pleasant, the little town in central Utah where I was born and spent my first fifteen years. I don't remember when I got my first library card, but I do remember my frustration that the librarian, who was a sweet young lady, but a stickler for the rules, would not let me check out more than one book at a time, while I could read two or three books in an evening. This was in the depth of the great depression, when pennies were scarce, but somehow my parents found a way to get their five children whatever they needed. My older brother learned to play a clarinet, and when I was in the third grade I got and learned to play a well-worn e flat alto saxophone. That saxophone fits into a rather large case, so after school, on days when we weren't playing football on the church lawn, which was next to the library, I used to take the sax home, leave the sax on my bed, take the empty case to the library, and when the librarian wasn't watching, fill the case up with books, check one out, take them all home, read them, then, in a day or two, bring them back and do it again. By the time I'd finished sixth grade I had read most of the books in the library. It wasn't large. I did have a problem, though. One day my older sister—she was seven years older than I—picked up the book I was reading at the moment and went screaming to my mother that I was reading 'dirty' books. It was Aldous Huxley's "Brave New World" and it contained a line about bare-breasted women listening to music in a science-fiction type of entertainment center. I was all in favor of such entertainment centers, but my sister, who happened to open it to that page, was horrified. The librarian, of course, would not have checked out that book to a sixth grade boy, but the book had gone out in my saxophone case, and she knew nothing about it. My mother made me put it back in the same way, which I would have done by myself, of course, but that pretty much ended my book smuggling. I didn't care much. I'd read most of the books in the library by then and needed a wider selection. Fate conspired to help me. My brother, Don, after high school, entered B.Y.U. (Brigham Young University) in Provo, fifty miles north of our little town of Mt. Pleasant. He completed two years there just as I completed junior high school, in Mt. Pleasant. It wasn't a large school. The senior high and the junior high, with the gymnasium, were together in one medium sized building. The junior high and the gymnasium occupied most of the first floor, and the senior high and the auditorium occupied most of the second floor, with a band (music) room off in one corner. Our father taught science in a room on the second floor. In those days the winter snows were so deep that the only way I could get to school on the snowed in streets in the morning was to follow in my father's footsteps as he walked to the high school. From there the streets were usually snowplowed to the elementary school, so I could get on to school by myself. I varied this, occasionally, by attaching a harness to Prince, my collie, so that he could pull my sled over the snow to school, with me on it. When we'd reach the school, I'd say, "Go home, Prince." He would pull the empty sled home and my mother would unhook him. I never could figure out how to have him come get me after school, but the streets had had enough foot traffic by that time so that I could walk home. The snow was high enough so that it covered most of the fences on the fields surrounding the town. Our neighbor put his farm wagon on runners in the winter, so that it became a bobsled. On late afternoons and evenings he would fill the sled with neighborhood kids and we'd bobsled over the fields, bundling under blankets and singing songs. I got my first kiss, other than from my mother, under those blankets, but I was so young that I didn't know what to do with it, sadly, and it was wasted.

There is a point to this story---how I came to be in Los Angeles to finish high school, to be drafted, to find my way to the Air Corps, and to join the storied 91st in the bloodiest conflict of all time.

When my brother finished his two years of pre-med at BYU he somehow managed to get himself admitted to the dental school at USC, in Los Angeles. How he did that we never knew, except that when I asked him, in later years, he said that he'd looked at the people in our town. They were nearly all farmers, with a scattering of shopkeepers, a shoemaker, a barber (although only the well-to do used the barber) and similar people. Most of the men grew beards or shaved themselves, and once a month we brothers endured the hair-pulling that resulted as our father used the clippers to keep our hair short enough to comb. The trapper that my father and the other sheepmen hired to keep the coyote population in check (to keep our sheep alive) lived a block from us. There was one doctor, and one dentist. Don said that he'd looked at how the people of the town lived. The dentist seemed to live better than most, so Don decided he would do that, too, having some skill with his hands, developed by whittling during the long summers when he was alone with a herd of sheep and a pocket knife. When he was about to finish his second year at BYU, he applied to the USC dental school, and was accepted. When the sheepherding need evaporated, after the crash of '29, he worked for the railroad, laying track, in the summer, to earn money to live on in Los Angeles, eventually. When the time came for him to leave for Los Angeles, he said "Goodby" to our grandmother, with whom he'd lived during his two years at the "Y", sleeping in the hall on a cot, where I replaced him, later—Our grandmother was quite old. She'd raised 12 children on a hardscrabble farm near Mt. Pleasant, lost her husband to pneumonia when the children were half grown, and moved to a home in Provo, where she rented half of the house to roomers and lived in the other half. That's quite a story. She came from Norway by herself, with her mother, when she was twelve—but I'll tell that story later, if I have the time and if you're interested.

My grandmother never learned English, or at least not enough to communicate with, so I learned a little Norwegian, which, sadly, I promptly forgot when I left Provo.

Don made an arrangement with a college friend's father, who was to drive a truck load of lumber to Los Angeles, to ride in the truck, on the lumber, to Los Angeles. So Don rode his bicycle to Mt. Pleasant, where he was to meet the truck, and waited, and waited, and waited. When it was apparent that the truck was not coming, he made a tiny trailer, put his suitcase and a blanket on it and set out for Los Angeles. He rode that bicycle across the 800 miles of Utah, Arizona, Nevada and California to Los Angeles, entered the Dental School, got a night job working in a glass factory to earn room and eating money, began a lifelong attachment to the USC football team by playing his clarinet in the S.C. marching band and began his dental training. It was a hard life. He completed his first year, but in the middle of the second year an uncle who hadn't heard from him for some time went to find him. He found him, in his lonely room, unconscious and dying of pneumonia. The uncle called the parents in Utah, told them Don was dying, and said they'd better come down for the funeral. Our parents, who were both teaching, left their jobs, picked me up from where I'd been living with my grandmother in Provo, sleeping in the bed Don had vacated, bundled in their two younger boys, and drove to Los Angeles for the funeral. Don wasn't quite dead. The relative had put him in a hospital in intensive care, and Don, who'd always been a survivor, hung on. Our parents took him out of the hospital, found an empty house, opened a boarding house in it to pay their way and nursed Don back to health. It took the rest of the year, but USC gave him a leave. He redid the year the next year, with the Army paying his tuition--Pearl Harbor had occurred and the war was on. He completed his schooling and became a dentist, but since they had paid for his last two years of dental school he belonged to the army. After MacArthur invaded the Phillipines and drove up the islands, Don was sent to an advanced unit which needed a dentist. The Japanese were well on their way to defeat, but there were still a few of their soldiers lurking in the wilds near the Americans' camp. One day, after long hours of work with a foot pedal supplying the power for his dental drill, Don went to his tent to nap for a while. Just as he lay down, a Japanese hidden on the edge of the camp, but with a working machine gun, loosed a burst toward the Americans' tents. Don's tentmate, who was standing near his cot, was cut in two, but Don who was lying down, wasn't hit. He was still surviving.

 I worked in my parents' boarding house, which at first was near U.S.C., so I enrolled at the nearby high school, Polytechnic, and enjoyed the big city. When my parents found a more munificent house, in the Wilshire District, I rode the streetcar across town to continue at Poly. I had been in a very small high school in Mt. Pleasant, then in a somewhat larger high school in Provo, but in each town there was only one high school. When I enrolled at Poly I assumed that, as in the other schools I'd been in, there was only one high school in the city, so when we moved to the Wilshire district I continued at Poly, assuming it was the only high school in town. I'd done a lot of running up and down mountains when herding sheep with my father, and at that time my father still held the college record for running the mile, in Utah, so I ran the mile at Poly in Los Angeles.

Why I didn't realize, as we competed against L.A. High and other schools, that I might enroll at a school closer to our then home, I don't know. But it was fortunate that I didn't. Poly was a good school and I was happy there—and there were big libraries nearby. I had pretty well exhausted the library in Provo while I was there. Since my grandmother had had to pinch pennies all of her life, she made sure that all of the lights were turned off when darkness came at the end of the day. There was no way for me to study or read there, so I walked up to the city library every evening and studied there. And looking through the stacks I found authors I'd never heard of. I discovered Edgar Rice Burroughs and spent many evenings with John Smith on Mars, and Tarzan and others in their many adventures. Willa Cather I could sympathize with. I'd spent many a freezing day keeping my father's sheep alive.

I'd missed the friends I grew up with in Mt. Pleasant when I moved to Provo. And I missed the new friends I'd made at Provo when I left so abruptly for Los Angeles. It wasn't so easy to make friends in Los Angeles. Big schools are much more impersonal than small schools. When we went back to a school reunion in Mt. Pleasant fifty years after I'd left it, my wife was amazed that I knew almost every one of the people who attended—most of whom had never left the vicinity of that small town. And I knew the history of almost every house in the town and the families that lived in them. My grandfather, as a boy, had been the bugler who blew the bugle for Indian attacks from the wall of the then fort, where now there was a high school. Then I made a new set of friends in the service, but they were almost all killed, and I started over again making friends after the war.

I've said, above, that my father was one of twelve children raised on a hardscrabble farm in a tiny town in central Utah. There was no high school near when he finished elementary school, so he went to Salt Lake City, lived with a married sister who lived in Salt Lake, and finished high school there. He never talked to us about his life there, but he must have been a gifted track athlete. He entered the A.C. (Utah State Agricultural College). There was absolutely no money and as far as we know there was no such thing as an athletic scholarship in those days, so he joined the ROTC, (we have pictures of him in his ROTC uniform) to earn his way, and did professional wrestling in the little towns around for living money. He and his roommate (who later became an M.D.) would go up to a little town in Idaho (or anywhere), Dad would put on a turban and be the big bad infidel from abroad, and the local hero (the roommate) would win the match, then they would go down into Utah, where the roommate would be the big, bad infidel and Dad the local hero, who, after a wild wrestling match, would defeat the infidel and take the prize money. Meanwhile, back at the university, Dad was setting track records. He set a college mile record in Utah that lasted for more than a decade. He did the same in the 880, but it didn't last so long. One of my earliest memories is of a time when my mother was out of town. There was a Gypsy camp in the meadow below town and they came into town and challenged the townspeople to produce a champion who would wrestle their trained bear. (A muzzle on the bear and claws clipped, but still enormously powerful). Knowing of my father's college wrestling exploits, the townspeople persuaded my father to accept the Gypsy challenge. One of my aunts preserved a newspaper column which describes the match. It says "Andy backed up as the bear advanced, then he moved in, grabbed the bear's forepaw and flipped the bear over his shoulder. The bear refused to wrestle any further. Andy took the disappointed Gypsy's money, and the Gypsys left town." I was six years old, but I have a vivid memory of that bear. This story is so incredible, my father wrestling and defeating a full grown bear, that I've put a local newspaper account of the proceedings on the next page of this account.

One other story of that superb man, my father. When he still had his sheepherds, when I was quite a young boy, seven or eight years old, in the early spring, when the sheep were brought in from the desert where they had wintered, they were kept in fields just outside of town while they lambed (gave birth to their lambs). Some of those winters were very cold, with icy blizzards as late as May, when the sheep had very young lambs, so Don and I were kept out of school, when necessary, to keep the sheep moving, so they, especially the lambs, would not freeze. I can remember riding my horse among the sheep to keep them moving, then when the schoolday was over and my father came out to relieve me, riding my horse home, unsaddling, putting the horse in the barn, feeding him (usually a her) and going inside to run cold water over my hands to ease the frostbite which was just setting in.

Page Twelve — The Pyramid   ember 13, 1979

It happened in Sanpete

The night of the bear

By Morris Olsen

When I was just a kid, some gypsies camped in a field below Mount Pleasant. They had a large bear with them, secured by a chain, and we would walk down there to marvel at this huge animal.

One night, my father said to me: Morris, do you want to see Andy Anderson wrestle a bear? "Why, of course," I answered.

We went to the old Armory hall by the movie house. Andy was clad in tights -- a blocky, hirsute man, who had become famous as a wrestler at ~~Brigham Young~~ University. USA College.

The bear entered the ring on a leash, held by the gypsy, who had prudently muzzled him. He was a hulking beast with a prima donna temperament, which surfaced when the gypsy told boys in the encircling audience to remove their hats. (The bear doesn't like to see people wearing hats in the building.)

They laughed at him. The bear growled and lunged, with the gypsy straining at the leash. Those hats came off in unison!

This caused the bear's opponent to reevaluate his decision to wrestle this unpredictable animal. He made a most cautious approach. The bear stood up and they shook hands. His timidity prevented him from closing to get an effective hold. Finally, the bear reached out with a paw, spun Andy around and encircled him with his front legs. The audience tensed and there were whispers of "look - he's getting the bear hug on him."

This was supposed to be the grand finale and to spell finis: Not so. Andy threw his arms behind his head clutched the bear's fur, dropped to his knees, and tumbled the bear over his head, across the floor. At the same instant, he appeared to lose his fear, and in the ensuing clash between man and monster he soon had the bear pinned to the mat, to the accompaniment of threatening growls.

The gypsy raised Andy's hand in victory, saying this was only the second time the bear had been pinned. Then he consoled the bear, who behaved like he wanted to say, "Papa, I've just sold the farm." But Andy and the bear shook hands again and remained friends. Andy also acquired a new name From then on, he was known as "Andy Bear Wrestler."

Reader likes bear story

Editor, Pyramid:

Two weeks ago a short article on Andy Anderson fighting a bear was printed in The Pyramid.

Mr. Anderson was my uncle and that is the best account I've ever heard or read of. I was so happy to have it.

Sincerely,
Dorothy J. Buchanan

When the weather was a little warmer and the lambs a little older we would trail the sheep up into the mountains to our families' combined homestead lands (and rented government forest grazing land). The mountainous area where we took our sheep to graze was far from any roads, so we packed our tent and supplies on a pack horse and lived in the tent for weeks at a time, my father and me with one herd, and Don with another herd a few miles away. Coyotes love to eat sheep, and they hunt at dawn, so my father would roll out of bed just before down, go out to guard the sheep, then, after sunrise, when the sheep were grazing peacefully, return to wake me, cook breakfast, and embark on our daily activities. One day I woke after sunrise. My father had not returned, and for a long time, he did not return. I was quite young, too young to saddle up a horse and go looking for my father, so I just waited—and worried. In the middle of the morning my father dragged himself in, looking completely exhausted—I'd never seen him so worn. After he'd rested a while and had some food he was able to tell me what had happened to him. We had bedded the sheep down on a small flat on the mountainside. There was a mountain spring (water) at one end of the flat, which was one reason why we had bedded them down there, so they could drink. Growing beside the spring was a growth of chokecherries---and the berries, though too bitter for us to eat, were attractive to berry eating animals. Behind the chokecherry bush, with a small cub beside her was a bear. As my father walked around the chokecherry bush, he came face to face with the bear, which was stretching up to her full height to eat the chokecherries. When my father came around the bush, he almost tripped over the cub. When the bear saw my father standing over the cub, she came at him. Bears ordinarily amble at a leisurely pace, but when irritated or angry, they can move at unbelievable speed. This bear, in defense of her cub, came like a freight train. Dad turned, took off on the trail down the mountain, and ran, he said, like he'd never run before. The trail, worn by deer and an occasional horse, like ours, wound down the mountain for several miles. Dad said he could hear the pounding of that animal's feet right behind him all the way down the mountainside. Eventually, totally exhausted, he stopped and turned around to face the bear. There was no bear. The sounds he could hear were from his dog, following him down the trail, the same collie dog, Prince, that I trained, in the wintertime, to pull me to school on my sled.

The bear wrestling is fuzzy in my very young memory, and I don't know what happened when my mother returned. Life returned to normal, I suppose. When the careening markets of the late 1920s ended in the financial disaster of 1929, my grandfather and father struggled on for a few years, then they lost their homestead land and their herds to the bank and my father took a job as coach at the local high school. His principal job was teaching science, however, and when the vagaries of athletic success impelled the district to hire a new coach, Dad became a full time science teacher and what would now be called an athletic coordinator. I remember him slipping me in the door when he was taking tickets to the local all-stars' basketball contest with the Harlem Globetrotters. (Yes, there was a touring Harlem Globetrotters team that far back). It was a spine-tingling contest, of course, with the Globetrotters always coming out a few points ahead.

In the spring of 1938 Dad put some wooden hoops over the back of his half-ton truck, stretched canvas over them to make what was a motorized prairie schooner, put mother in the front seat with him, his three boys who were still home (Don was laying track from the railroad in the western desert to earn money for his coming college expenses, and my sister was teaching) in the back, and drove to the west coast to collect marine specimens for his science classes. He put the ocean artifacts he found into jars of formaldehyde to preserve them, took them back to his classroom and used them in his science teaching. There were no other such things in local schools, of course, but Dad was always one step ahead in his science teaching. I remember, when I was several years younger and we still had a herd of sheep, while driving that herd up into the mountain country where they were to summer, at night putting the herd onto a small corner of land surrounded by a creek, sleeping across the only access spot so that they couldn't get by at night---there was no electricity or auto light within fifty miles, so the stars seemed just beyond our reach, and Dad pointing out the constellations and musing on how they were formed, their age, and their relationship to the rest of our universe.

Dad was the middle one of his parents' twelve children, and the only one to get to a college until the very last one, who made it on athletics, as I suppose my father did. Ken was an All-American in basketball at BYU. I suppose the oldest brother, John, was an inspiration to them. He was a national champion AAU wrestler and taught wrestling for years in Salt Lake City at the YMCA. That's aside from my story, though, except that it helps to explain how I got to Los Angeles. Dad would never talk about it to his children. I suppose he didn't want them to lose their faith, but in the fall of 1939 the school board, composed largely of good Mormons of Mt. Pleasant, where I had grown up, so far, didn't renew my father's teaching position. His teaching of evolution in his science classes was the impelling reason, I'm sure, because for years I met people who told me what an inspiring teacher my father was—and evolution was anathema to the Mormon doctrine of that time. I am grateful that those fine people have progressed to the point where they now generally accept the scientific tenets of evolution. But at that time the depression of the late 20s and the 30s had demolished his sheep business, and my grandfather, on my mother's side, who had been my father's backer and partner, had just died, so Dad found a job teaching in a school in eastern Utah, in Carbon County, and moved his family there. My brother, Don, had just left on his bicycle for his dental school, USC, in California, so I went to Provo to help care for my other grandmother, sleeping in the space which Don had left. We weren't told, of course, why my father had taken his family from the central Utah agricultural town of Mt. Pleasant, to the coal mining country of Carbon County, in eastern Utah, and I remained an active member of the L.D.S. (Mormon) church.

My father could do almost anything with his hands. When I came home from my combat days I moved from station to station as I did various things. Transportation was hard to find. No automobiles were to be found, of course. The plants which had made autos had been making tanks for several years, and there simply were no autos for sale. There were, however, some new, unused auto engines stored in warehouses. Dad was able to buy one of these. He found an old, used auto body, took the worn-out engine out of it, and put the new one in. Then he gave it to me as a coming home present, so for the rest of the war, and through my college years, I was able to drive from station to station and travel as I needed to during college. And I stayed a member of the Mormon group of young people at UCLA. Good people, a little insular, and bound by the strictures of their faith. I found what was meant by the phrase I heard in one of my philosophy classes, "Faith is a powerful thing. It often shuts off the rational mind"

Mormons, as are most other thoughtful, church-going people, are generous, kind, caring people, but their theology leaves something to be desired.

Years later, after I had left the Air Force and entered U.C.L.A. I was elected president of the L.D.S. social group at U.C.L.A., called Lambda Delta Sigma. We maintained social contact with similar groups at other universities in the state. It was at a time of unrest throughout the country, largely because of the blatant racial discrimination which was almost universal in the United States at that time, to which the Mormon church at that time was a heavy contributor, because it excluded black people from the Mormon religious hierarchy (the "priesthood") to which all male Mormons belonged. The reason given for this stand by the church leadership was that, according to the teachings given to them, by religious writings and by church doctrine, was that in the councils in heaven in a previous life, Satan, who was a son of God, as all spirits were, had rebelled against the leadership of God. In the resultant struggle Satan was ejected from the fellowship who supported the teachings of God and banished from their company. Those spirits who had not supported God were allowed to stay in his company, but when it came their time to obtain a mortal body and experience life on earth before returning to the presence of God (after death) they would be cursed with a black skin. I know this sounds ridiculous, but it was the actual doctrine taught in Mormonism as we who were in college then were growing up. It was so silly that we leaders of the LDS groups at the various colleges in California agreed to call a conference of our groups to discuss the matter, and to then refer our conclusions to the leaders of the church in Salt Lake City. We arranged our conference in Fresno. As we opened our conference, one of the church leaders form Salt Lake City appeared. He said we had no right to discuss such matters, we were in an illegal meeting, such doctrinal discussion could only be held under the guidance and leadership of authorities in Salt Lake City. He pronounced the conference closed and told us to take ourselves back to our homes. Then he walked out. We were appalled, but the church facilities which were hosting us were locked against us, and since we had no other resources, we went back to where we came from. Church doctrine did not change. Many of those young people left the church. I did not, because so much of my family background and history had been a part of the church, and I thought that the only way to change the church was to work from within to make those changes. Later, at UCLA, in reading the works of John Milton in our studies of literature, I realized that the story of the council in heaven and the expulsion of a part of the group was the story Milton created in "Paradise Lost." How Joseph Smith, the Mormon prophet and leader, became familiar with that story is beyond me, but he did, and it became a part of Mormon lore, and thus a problem for those of us who hated the culture of segregation which the LDS church at that time espoused and which all believing members were forced to accept. Thank God that nonsense is no longer taught as a part of the Mormon gospel and culture.

Years later, when an inner city school, almost all black student body and faculty, was falling apart, and I was sent by the district to try to bring it back to life, a Black Panther group tried to rally the community against me by informing the community that I was a Mormon, and as a result, believed in the inferiority of Blacks, which made me an inadequate school leader in a Black community. I informed the community that I had fought against that false doctrine all of my adult life, that I had not left the church because the best way to change is from within, and that I would continue to try to effect that change. The black community, bless their hearts, rallied round me, supported what I was trying to do, and eventually, when I requested a transfer to be nearer my home, asked if I would stay to continue the work that we had begun. I have always regretted that I did not stay, but I was exhausted. The job was daylight to dark, a long, long drive, and I had missed three years of much of my children's lives. I did retain many friends from that time, however, one of whom was Tom Bradley, the then City Councilman and later the long time mayor of Los Angeles. It was a time when a professor in the east was proclaiming that marijuana was an enhancer of life, a doctrine highly destructive to young people, so quite often I would ask our local city councilman, who was Tom Bradley, to come talk to our students about the real evils of marijuana and other drugs. He always did and because of his character and position, our students trusted him, so he was believed and did a great deal of good. Later I was able to offer help and support to him and we remained life-long friends. It was he who had the city 'scrollmaker' make the illuminated scroll from the city which I took to our friends in France when we were able to visit them. And when Tom called me, one day, said, "Andy, I'm establishing a 'Commission On The Status Of Women' as a part of the government of Los Angeles. I need a man on it. Would you be that man?" Of course I said, "Yes," so I drove downtown once a month for those commission meetings for five years. And I believe the commission did a lot of good, although we had some fierce arguments about what needed to be done to promote the welfare of women in government in the city of Los Angeles. Sometimes I was overwhelmed—the Commission consisted of six militant women and me—but I found that those ladies were right more often than not, and I was able to be of some help, and provide some gender support. And I was constantly able to see what a great man that first black mayor of Los Angeles was. I have always been proud that we were friends.

But those are stories that belong in another book. Now back to that dreadful war, and the brilliant part which the 91st Heavy Bombardment Group and its support groups played in it.

I was led into the above account by telling the story of my father, what happened to him, and, as a result, what happened to me. But now, back to my story (all real life) of the war. I'm the luckiest man in the world to be alive, and I know it. Remember, at the beginning of this account I related that of the first 36 planes and crews that arrived in England in the 91st Heavy Bombardment Group, 38 were lost. And that, a year later, when I flew, we lost 32 of our 36 ships in the time that I flew. When I returned to my Group, after being gone for a relatively brief time, there were few faces left that I knew. The 91st was the best group in the 8th Air Force, but there are many other men who will tell you that they flew with the best group—their group. There were many of those groups. There were 42 heavy bomber groups, 4 medium bomber groups, 20 fighter groups, and 50 support groups based in England. Those were American forces. The British had their own units, as brave and as skilled (almost) as ours. Those American groups flew 330 thousand bomber sorties, dropped over 680 thousand tons of bombs, and destroyed nearly sixteen thousand enemy aircraft. They were awarded 17 Congressional Medals of Honor, 226 Distinguished Service Crosses, more than 440,000 Air Medals, and countless other awards. The 8th Air Force had 26,000, that we know of, killed, more than 7,000 wounded, over 30 thousand prisoners of war, and more than 1500 internees.

The 91st had the highest total of enemy aircraft destroyed of any group—420. We had the highest losses of any 8th Air Force group—197. We were the first Group to attack a target in the Ruhr, the March 4, 1943, mission to Hamm—(which I really will get to in a minute). The 91st led the famous Schweinfurt mission of August 17, 1943, the purpose of which was to destroy the ball-bearing production capacity of the Reich. We were the first 8th Air Force group to complete 100 missions---January 5th, 1944. We were the first to test flak suits—in March of 1943. We, with others, flew the last combat mission of the war---to Pilsen, on April 25, 1945, and we flew the largest rescue mission ever, to Poland, to bring out long-term prisoners of war, including many from our own group, some of whom I met via our computer correspondence in later years.

Now back to that 22nd mission, the first mission deep into the heartland of Germany, and one which said to the German Luftwaffe, and flak battalions, "Here we come. Try and stop us." 'Wake-up' that morning was at 4:00 a.m. Breakfast at 5:00, briefing at 6:00. Take-off scheduled for 8:00, and they took off on time, heading for Hamm, a marshalling yard city deep in the Ruhr Valley, four and a half hours away. The 91st had flown two missions in the previous week----to the docks at Wilhelmshaven on February 26th, and to the sub pens at Brest on the 27th. Both were strenuous missions. Short Snorter II and Kickapoo were lost on the 26th, and though there were no losses, the mission to Brest on the 27th was a difficult one, with considerable damage to several planes. As a result, only 20 planes were available for the mission to Hamm on March 4th, and four of those planes aborted early in the mission, due to mechanical problems. When the cover was raised on the map on stage, and the long, red line leading to Hamm, in the Ruhr Valley, was revealed, silence reigned in the briefing room. It was the first mission that deep into the heart of the German homeland. It was to be a long, difficult day. The 102nd Combat Wing was assigned to lead the mission, with the 303rd Group in the lead. The 101st Combat Wing, comprised of the 306th, as the lead group, and the 91st, followed, with Major Paul Fishburne, the 22 year old commander of the 322nd squadron, later my squadron, leading the way.

The 91st took off as scheduled, at 0800 hours, joined the rest of the Strike Force, and headed out over the North Sea. The Strike Force almost immediately encountered what soon became almost total cloud cover, consisting of three cloud layers between 13,000 and 17,000 feet. Above these was another layer of clouds extending from 21,500 feet to 26,000 feet. Visibility soon dropped to less than 1000 yards. The 102 Combat Wing, judging conditions would not improve, diverted south, to clear skies and Rotterdam, where they dropped on their secondary targets, German airfields. The 306th Group, now out of touch with the 91st because of the heavy cloud cover, aborted back to England. Because radio silence had been maintained and because the heavy cloud cover made visual contact impossible, Major Fishburne was unaware that the other groups had abandoned the mission, and that the 91st was proceeding on alone.

At the before dawn briefing, the weather officer, Major Lawrence Atwell, had told the crews that they would find dense cloud conditions over the North Sea, but that conditions would improve as they approached the continent, and the target would be clear. As predicted, the lower cloud layer diminished to about 5/10 cover near the coast. Fishburne had assumed that the other Group in his Combat Wing and the Groups of the other Wing, the 102nd, had done as he had done, flown through the clouds on instruments, and were now ready to brave the German defense over the continent. He asked his tail gunner to make a sight check and tell him how many planes were still in the attack formation. The gunner answered, "16, sir." Fishburne asked him to check again. He had set out with 20 planes.

Four had aborted because of engine problems, but because they had been ordered to observe strict radio silence, and they had been flying in moderately thick cloud cover, Fishburne was not aware of the abortions. That left him with 16 planes, but as far as he knew, the two Groups of the 102nd Wing were still with him. He asked the tail gunner to look again. The tail gunner did, and said, "Still 16, sir." Fishburne had no way of knowing that the Groups of the 102nd Wing had aborted and gone off to bomb the German airfields near Rotterdam. Because of the orders to observe strict radio silence, he also did not know that the other group of his Combat Wing, the 306th, believing that the heavy cloud cover would force the aborting of the mission, had aborted, also, and returned home with their bombs secured. When the 306th Group and the Groups of the 102nd Wing were not visible, he assumed they would catch up with him, so he went on his way to bomb the rail marshalling yards at Hamm, deep in the flak and fighter protected interior of Germany.

As he crossed the German border, Fishburne again asked his tail gunner how many ships were in formation, including their own. The answer, again, was "16, sir." Now Fishburne had a hard decision to make. It was the policy of the 8th Air Force at this time that small groups of unescorted bombers not go deep into enemy territory. And this was a wise policy. A small group could bring only a limited number of guns to bear on an attacking force, while a large group, such as the two Wing, four group force that they had begun with, would have a firepower of more than 800 fifty caliber machine guns to discourage fighter attacks. Their small group would carry roughly 60,000 pounds of explosives, while the larger group would have carried at least 240,000 pounds, enough to blast any marshalling yard out of existence, providing the bombing was on target, which it sometimes was and sometimes wasn't, in those days, depending on the flak and fighter defenses and the accuracy of the bomb aimers. Fishburne had a choice. He would have been justified in aborting, turning back. Rather than the eighty to a hundred bombers that they had begun with, they now had 16. Rather than the roughly 800 machine guns to deter fighter attacks, they now had 160. The odds were now not in his favor, but his orders had been to bomb the marshalling yards. It appeared that the weather over the target was now clear. German fighters had not yet appeared. He decided to follow the last orders he had heard. They flew on.

When the strike force, over the North Sea, had split up and flown in different directions, the German air defense controller was confused. It appeared that the major strike was to be in the area of Rotterdam, but one part of the force had reversed itself and returned to England. German air defense did not determine the final direction of the attack until the 91st was thirty minutes from their target, but then all Hell broke loose. More than 175 fighters came at the 91st for the next hour. Me 109s, FW 190s, ME 110s, and Ju 88s attacked the bombers in a constant stream, sometimes singly, sometimes two or three abreast, in line or in trail. The attacks were low and high, front and rear, and at various angles. Anti-craft batteries began to get their range. Flak over the target was intense and accurate, but the target was clear. They turned off the I.P. onto the bomb run in a tight formation and began an almost textbook perfect approach. The bomb pattern was one of the best in the Group's history. The clear weather allowed them a good view, and the marshalling yard was almost destroyed. In confirmation, three days later, photo reconnaissance flights brought back photos of a devastated marshalling yard, with buildings destroyed, tracks obliterated, and freight cars in ruins littering the area. But the Group paid a heavy price. Four of the sixteen ship formation were destroyed. Number 512, "Rose-o-day," was hit by fighters, and after a prolonged, vicious battle crashed in the North Sea. "Stupen-taket," of the 322nd, was hit by flak and exploded in mid-air over the target. Two 324th planes, "Excalibur" (# 464) and # 370 (no name) were so badly damaged that they crashed (ditched) in the North Sea. The radio operator on 070, "Invasion 2nd," was killed in the air, and almost every plane received heavy flak or fighter damage. On the other hand, the "Daily Reports" of the 323rd squadron for March 4th reported that planes from that squadron shot down four German attackers. A Lt. Fisher was credited with an Me 109, Tech Sgt. Remmel shot down an Me 110, and S/Sergeants Streets and Perri each shot down one FW 190. There were undoubtedly other claims made, but I can find no record of them. There is a record, however, of what happened to those remarkable warplanes which survived that memorable mission to the Hamm marshalling yards.

Two were shot down on the April 17th (1943) raid to Halle (Bremen). They were two of the six lost that day, the entire 401st squadron. The six were "Rain of Terror", "Short Snorter III", "Sky Wolf II," "Thunderbird", "Hellsapoppin" and "Invasion II".

It was a sad day for the 91st, but the decision had been made to continue the long missions, and the 8th Air Force (and the 91st) stuck with it. Four more of that "Hamm 16" were lost in that disastrous, but necessary, mission to Schweinfurt on August 17th to destroy the German ballbearing plants. It was a bloody day. The 401st again lost two ships, "Frank's Nightmare" and "Hitler's Gremlin." The 324th lost two ships, "Great Speckled Bird," and "Our Gang." The 321st lost "Stup-n-takit," "Stormy Weather" and "The Eagle's Wrath," and the 322 lost "My Prayer," "Chief Sly II," "Dame Satan" and "The Bearded Lady." Eleven ships and their crews gone, that day, from the 91st alone. Scores from other groups.

Another of the 12 was lost on a mission to Kiel, "Hell's Angles" of the 322 on May 14th, and "Shooting Star" was lost on a mission to Stuttgart on September 6, 1943. "Shooting Star" was damaged over the target and as a result was forced to ditch in the English Channel on the return flight. One man was killed before the ditching, but the remaining nine stayed afloat in the icy water by clinging to the one raft which remained usable. They were in the sea for several hours, but finally an ASR (Air-sea-rescue) craft came along to pick them up. Lloyd Shaper, the pilot, reported that all nine were still alive when the ASR came into sight, but three succumbed to exhaustion and cold, and in spite of their companions' efforts to hold them up, slipped into the sea at the last minute, and were lost, leaving six survivors. One more of the Hamm survivors, "Green Fury," was shot down on the October 9th mission to Anklam. They were not alone. The 91st lost five other ships that day, two from the 323rd and three from the 322nd squadrons.

Of the last three planes from that historic mission, one has been lost in the mists of time, one was transferred to another Group and also lost to record, and the last, so battle-worn that she could hardly fly, was stripped of armaments, transferred to the "Aphrodite" program and loaded with explosives so that she could be flown, pilotless, on August 43, 1944, to destroy a V-bomb site, in France, which she did.

The valor and skill of the 91st, and of the 8th Air Force as a whole, were proved on that mission to Hamm, if they needed proving. The deep penetration of the German heartland had been accomplished, the bombing aim and pattern had been almost perfect, the marshalling yard and its contents were reduced to scrap, a number of German fighters had been destroyed, and the planning and instructions given the airmen were successfully carried out. Nevertheless, the generals at higher headquarters were not happy with Major Fishburne. He had continued alone deep into the continent with a small force, with no fighter protection. Indeed, fighters with that extended range were not yet available in quantity, so there had been no effort to provide effective fighter cover, but the B-17s had gone deep into the 'enemy heartland,' destroyed an essential and irreplaceable German resource, and returned a majority of the attacking force safely. Again, what to do? Somewhat reluctantly, Major Fishburne was awarded the Distinguished Flying Cross for his valiant work that day, BUT he was reduced in rank to Captain and transferred to the 351st Bomb Group at Polebrook. There he was assigned as C.O. of the 509th Squadron and promoted back to Major. The 91st Bomb Group was awarded the Distinguished Unit Citation for its accomplishments that day, the first Bomb Group to be so designated. However, so as not to encourage other groups to go it alone deep into enemy territory, the DUC award was not made known until two years following the end of the war. What nonsense! The generals in command didn't have enough good sense or foresight to see what a morale boost the story of this Group and its leader's skill and bravery would have, both in the Air Force and in the nation back home, if it were publicized rather than being hidden. Major Fishburne completed his tour of missions and returned home. When the results of the Hamm mission were reported to Churchill and Roosevelt, skepticism regarding the soundness of high altitude precision bombing, as was done on March 4th by the 91st, abated. So the mission was a major factor in deciding to continue the daylight bombing, which the 8th Air Force and the 91st did, with a vengeance, and which shortened the war, with its tragic personnel and materiel losses, immeasurably. The 'Distinguished

Unit Citation' which was awarded for the mission, but not made public until after the war, said:

Citation:

"The 91st Bombardment Group, of the 1st Bombardment Division (H), is cited for extraordinary heroism, determination, and esprit de corps in action against the enemy on 4 March, 1943. On this date the 91st Bombardment Group (H) took off from home base in England, as scheduled, to attack the railroad marshalling yards located at Hamm, Germany, in one of the first operations conducted by heavy bombardment units against targets within Germany. This unit departed the English coast on course and a few miles out over the English Channel encountered thick haze, high cloud, and icing conditions reducing visibility to less than 1000 yards. Weather conditions continued to deteriorate to such an extent that only the determination and skill of each pilot in maintaining formation was responsible for the negotiation of the flight across the English Channel. Three other bombardment groups comprising the force engaged in this military operation were forced to abandon the mission because of the adverse weather encountered. Over enemy-occupied Holland, weather conditions improved and the 91st Bombardment Group (H), consisting of sixteen B-17 aircraft, continued on toward the assigned objective. Vigorous attacks by enemy fighters began almost immediately. In the face of vicious opposition from an estimated 60 to 70 fighter airplanes of the German Air Force this unit demonstrated the utmost courage and determination, fighting doggedly to maintain course and position en route to the target. Although four B-17 aircraft were lost to enemy action and heavy anti-aircraft fire was met from enemy ground installations, the 91st Bombardment Group (H) successfully reached the marshalling yards at Hamm, Germany. In the face of opposition from enemy ground defenses, this unit tenaciously maintained the bomb run, and bombs were dropped, inflicting extensive damage on the German installations. The 12 surviving aircraft, having successfully completed their primary assignment, and having destroyed 13 enemy fighters, probably destroyed another 3 and damaged 4, continued to maintain formation integrity, and completed the return flight to home base. The conspicuous courage and esprit de corps exhibited by the 91st Bombardment Group (H) in the face of extremely adverse weather conditions and opposition from the enemy, which resulted in casualties consisting of 1 killed, 5 seriously wounded, and 40 missing in action, were responsible for the successful bombardment of one of the first high priority objectives assigned to bombardment forces in the European Theater of Operations. The actions of this unit reflect the highest credit on the 91st Bombardment Group (H), and the armed forces of the United States. WDGO 29, 1947

Since a large part of this narrative is of my personal experiences, and since there is so much to tell about the 91st that I did not participate in, I recommend to you two books, "The Ragged Irregulars of Bassingbourn" by Marion Havelaar and William Hess, and, "The Ragged Irregulars, Memoirs of the 91st Bomb Group," written by many of us in the 91st, and published by the Turner Publishing Company, in Paducah, Kentucky. And you will find a number of books closely related to these two in the bibliography in the back of this book.

Now, back to the war and the 91st as I saw them. And if you're interested in seeing the war as another saw it, another valiant man, Sam Halpert, has written a novel you may like to read. It's "A Real Good War," published by Southern Heritage Press. Sam, a bombardier, arrived at the 91st just after I was shot down, and was lucky enough to fly a complete set of missions and come home alive. He recently put this piece of history on our website. I flew in the 322 squadron, and he flew in the 324th, but many of our missions were enough alike so that I'll put his story in here. Several of my missions were similar, although no two are really alike, and no one ever gets used to seeing his friends die. My third mission was a (relatively) low level mission to hit a German troop concentration and ammunition dump near St. Lo on July 24th. As far as I remember we only flew one low level mission again. The flak was too heavy and accurate at low level. Low level for us was about 12,000 ft. I remember looking back over my shoulder just in time to see one of my good friends, in a squadron just behind and to the right, catch a flak burst in the cockpit. No survivors.

A hard moment. We weren't up the next day, when they flew to the same target at the same altitude, but it was so rough that they never did it again. Now to Sam's story:

First, a word of explanation. Most of us 91sters who know each other, today, never knew each other while we were flying. While flying, we were grouped, both in living quarters and in training, into one squadron. Most of our time, while on the base, was occupied with actual combat or training for that combat. Training meetings, an occasional lecture on other subjects, some physical education time, usually spent in softball games, and letter writing—all of us wrote a lot of letters—occupied most of our time. We wrote letters, because if we wrote letters, we received letters, and any news or communication from family or friends meant concentration on something other than tomorrow's mission, where survival was questionable. I didn't play softball, I ran. I needed more of an energy outlet than softball provided, so I ran a lot. There was an officers' club and an enlisted man's club, where many of us spent what time we had to spare, but most of the time in the club was spent drinking beer, and since I had been raised a teetotaling Mormon, I never learned to like beer and I simply didn't drink other alcohol. Sex has always been a large part of wartime life for the men involved, and there was sex available. The first time I had spare time I went to the nearby little town of Royston, caught a bus to Cambridge, a few miles away, and caught a train from there to London, not a long journey. I found a room in a small hotel. It was the Hamilton, I believe, and went out to see the city. The part of the city that I could see, at first, was mostly women. The streets were full of them and most of them were not hesitant about accosting an unaccompanied Yank, especially one with officer's bars and wings. In Royston and in Cambridge, in the brief time we'd spent there, we'd frequently heard the British soldiers' complaint about Americans, that they were "overpaid, oversexed, and over here." The phrase was true, of course, although the pay scales, by today's standards, seemed pretty meager. The 1944 Air Force pay scales were:

Private: $ 50 monthly base pay
Private First Class: $ 54 monthly base pay
Corporal: $ 68 monthly base pay

Sergeant: $ 78 monthly base pay
Staff Sergeant: $98 monthly base pay
Technical Sergeant: $ 114 monthly base pay
Master Sgt.-First Sgt: $ 138 monthly base pay
Flight Officer: $ 1800/year base pay
Warrant Officer: $ 1800/year base pay
Chief Warrant Officer: $2100/year base pay
2nd Lieutenant: $1800/year base pay
1st Lieutenant: $ 2000/year base pay
Captain: $2400/year base pay
Major: $3000/year base pay
Lt. Colonel: $ 3500/year base pay
Colonel: $ 4000/year base pay
Brig. General: $ 6000/year base pay
Major General, Lt. General, and General: $ 8000 year base pay

In addition, most ranks received a 50% increase in flight pay if they flew regularly, and married soldiers received an allowance for dependents.

The average American soldier or airman was better dressed, had more money, and, it seemed, had a greater lust for women than his average British counterpart, so nature took its course. MPs were often busy in the clubs/pubs and sometimes on the streets separating Brits and Yanks, each of whom thought he was defending the honor of his group. We fliers had gone through a number of lectures, telling us this would be so, but hearing it and experiencing it were two different matters. When, a few steps out of my hotel, a pretty little thing stopped me, said "Buy me a drink, Yank? " I said "Sure," and did so. Then, when she said "Let's go," I said, "Where?" She said, "Wy, to my room." Then I grasped the fact that she was a "Piccadilly Commando," one of literally thousands of young English women who were making some spare money while their men were abroad. When I told her I would not give her money for her services and asked her why she did it, she said that she, and others like her, had had two choices. They were not skilled, so they could join a labor battalion and do farm work or do the same in a factory, or she could go to the city and do a service for the thousands of lonely men there. She was engaged to a soldier who was abroad, (and who didn't know what she was doing, I supposed, although I never asked), and she was saving the money she made so that when the war was over and her soldier returned, they could buy a farm, settle down, and raise a family. When she found that I would not provide money for sex, she said that she liked me, she'd like to stay and while away the day with me, but she had to make her quota for the day, so she'd better go seek someone else, which she did. Since the first few times that I visited London I stayed at the Hamilton, and it seemed that that was her territory, I saw her several times. Sometimes her roommate was with her, one of the most beautiful women I'd ever seen. She asked me, of course, if I wouldn't like to use her services. Her price was much higher than 'Bobby's since 'Bobby' was pretty enough, but not unusually so, but the roommate was a real beauty. Nature took its course as it always does. One day when I came to London and stopped at the bar which the two usually frequented, the roommate was there, but no 'Bobby'. When I asked about 'Bobby' the roommate told me that 'Bobby' had given an American a venereal disease. American M.P.s had picked her up, and she had never returned. The roommate had no way of finding out what Bobby's fate was, so she had found a new roommate, but she did miss Bobby, who was a sweet young thing.

When I was in Cambridge on an overnight pass I usually stayed at the Red Cross hostel, but since I had first stayed at the Hamilton and it was not expensive, I stayed there the first few times I came to London. And I am sharing this with you because most Americans have little or no comprehension of the agony the people of England, especially of its cities, went through. When the people of the British Empire, notably England, fought back instead of giving in easily as Hitler had thought they would after the Allied armies had been defeated in Europe, Hitler decided to teach them a lesson. He sent his warplanes to destroy the city of Coventry. Destroy it they did, literally. The city, the whole city, was blown to bits. Thousands were killed, but the British fighters were learning how to cope with the German onslaught. In the ongoing air battles so many German warplanes were destroyed that they abandoned the daylight bombing that had been so destructive. They developed, instead, what we called 'buzz-bombs,' which were simply single-winged boxes filled with explosives and with a propeller. There was no pilot. They were filled with just enough fuel to take them over the center of London. Then the engine stopped, the explosive loaded body dropped straight down and blew wherever it hit and its surroundings to rubble. The 'buzz-bomb' attack was in full strength while I was there. The buzz-bombs flew at night, because the British fighters could shoot them down in the daytime. The fighters could shoot them down at night, too, but it was more difficult. Radar was in its infancy and enough 'buzz-bombs' got through each night to keep the city in terror, and fire and rubble fighting forces always fully occupied. And because British fighters did shoot down many of the 'buzz-bombs,' Hitler's engineers developed what they called a V-I rocket. This was a rocket that was filled with explosive, then shot up in an upper-atmosphere reaching curve which came down on London with no sound preceding it, so it was not possible to shoot it down before it hit and created its devastation. One day, when I had a leave, I left the subway station, walked to the Hamilton House and tried the door. The door opened, but the door and a front wall were all that was left of the Hamilton House. Thereafter, when I visited London, I slept in the subway, with thousands of those valiant British citizens who remained in the city throughout its ordeal. The devastation in London was so great, however, that I didn't often go to London. Our navigator, Jack Swisher, and I became pretty good friends, and we often went, on our flight 'off' time into nearby Cambridge, to seek whatever we could find, mostly girls, since Jack wasn't much of a beer drinker, either, but he was a great girl collector and he led a very busy and colorful sex life. I wasn't so busy sexwise, partly because Jack and I went to a local dance, one night—sponsored, I believe, by the Red Cross. Two girls walked in. Jack asked one to dance and I the other. They had recently been brought from London to work in one of the local war industries and hadn't been courted yet by the girl seeking Americans. Kathleen and I hit it off, so from then on I usually went to Cambridge rather than London, while Jack went off on his own. Kathleen and I punted (rowed) on the river "Cam," explored the various parts of Cambridge University, which Kathleen had dreams of attending after the war. "Not likely, though" she said, because it then was an institution for men and no one could foresee the Western World emancipation of women which would begin after the war ended. I found a nurse at the base hospital to bicycle through the countryside with when Kathleen was busy and Kathleen saw other soldiers, but we became quite fond of each other.

I've said elsewhere that we all wrote a lot of letters because writing and receiving letters took our minds off tomorrow's mission. I didn't have a steady girl in high school, but since I went into the service soon after high school I began to meet women, with the possibility of serious attachment, at each of the bases I was sent to. The captain's sister that I escorted to the dance at Pre-flight I would have liked to keep in touch with, but in the bustle of leaving Pre-flight for Primary at Jackson, Mississippi, somehow I lost her address, and I never located her, again. Primary was so crammed with physical conditioning and learning to fly that there just wasn't much time for girl-seeking, but I used the dancing skills I'd practiced at Montgomery to dance with some of the girls who frequented the Red Cross in Cambridge. Kathleen became my favorite, though. After I escaped from Europe I was well treated by the intelligence community in London, and General Doolittle gave me a battlefield promotion to first lieutenant. We were kept in London for some time, with no news back at the base that we'd escaped, so when I got back, I went to Cambridge to let Kathleen know I'd survived. I got there at dusk. Before I rang the bell I looked in the window. Kathleen had another man (from another base) with her. I had a hard choice. At that time I didn't know yet that I wouldn't be allowed to fly combat again, and if I did, the mortality rate was so high that there was a better than fair chance that the same thing would happen again, so rather than put Kathleen through that strain, again, I didn't knock. I went back to the base. In a day or two I was re-assigned back to the Department of the Interior (the U.S), and never saw Kathleen again.

Back in the States I was pretty much given my choice of assignments, so I asked to be a flight instructor. Since I'd picked up flying fairly easily, I didn't realize how much training it took to become a competent instructor. I was given a month's leave at a rest home in California, but after a week I couldn't take the leisure any more, and asked to be returned to flying, so I was sent to Central

Instructors' School in San Antonio, where I was trained to be an 'Advanced' Instructor in B-25s. I instructed for a bit at La Junta, then at an 'Advanced' school at Bakersfield, California. The B-25 was an excellent plane, easy to fly, and dependable, but didn't quite provide the excitement I craved, so I wangled my way into the Ferry Command, which flew planes like the P-38 to areas from where they were sent to combat. Now that was fun. I don't remember ever being given a check-out flight in a P-38, but I guess I had one, because I spent the next few months flying them all over the United States for various reasons. And I'm telling you this because one day I took a P-38 into Jackson, Mississippi. I can't remember why, but I had an overnight there, so I caught a ride to the home of the girl from Jackson I'd been writing to, to take her out to dinner/dance/etc. We called a taxi to take us into town, and when it came, I opened the door for her. She frowned, said, "I can't ride in that car" and walked away. I said, "Why not?" She said, "There's a black man driving it." I don't remember how we got out to dinner. Maybe her father loaned me his car, but I never went back. That was the first time I'd become aware of the depth of the discrimination, if that's a strong enough word, in the South.

But I've strayed from my story of life in the 91st, again. I'll get back to it.

On the base we really didn't have a great deal of time off. Our Group commanders kept us busy learning new skills and refurbishing old ones in our small bits of leisure time, and we did training flights in our B-17s when we were not on actual combat duty. The weather in England is (was) so bad that more missions were called off than were flown, and it was highly frustrating to be called before daylight, briefed, load the plane for combat, often taxi to the flight line, and then have the mission called off because either the weather at Bassingbourn was too bad to take off, or the weather over Europe was too bad for us to bomb effectively. Compared to other Groups, though, we had it good. Most of the American bases in England were usually ankle deep in mud, with the crews shivering in Quonset huts. Bassingbourn had steam heat and concrete walks. I've always felt a bit guilty because the stories from other fliers of their daily lives were description of chills, coal stoves, and daily misery, while our lives at

Bassingbourn were usually quite comfortable. I asked my sister to send me a physiology book and I began to absorb it with thoughts of becoming a doctor after the war, but the torn bodies that we saw after almost every mission soon put that thought out of my head. And I really didn't have much time to plan a post-war life, especially since our mortality rate was so high that a post-war life, much of the time, seemed pretty problematical. Sex, at least the periphery of sex, was often in our thoughts, as it is in the minds of most young men, and the pressures we were under seemed to emphasize the importance of sex or the lack of it, in our lives. After my room-mate, another co-pilot, went down, his bunk was empty and my diary (a very brief and often skipped record) occasionally says, "Bob-(or someone else)-sleeping here tonight. His roommate has a girl in his room".

But those days were long ago and far away. And I have said that most of us who communicate today never knew each other while we were flying. We know each other only through the marvel of today's computer communication and a rare meeting of those of us who are left. And when we do meet, there aren't many of us, because we're scattered all over the world. While researching 91st records for this writing, I came across Sam Halpert's book, "A Real Good War." I read it and sent him a message, via computer, that I was proud of what he'd written. He'd read my story, on the 91st computer site, and he answered, saying, "Andy, your description of those frantic moments of combat is the best description of what we went through that I've ever read." Sam writes well. You readers with an interest in the events of those days would enjoy his book. He came to the 91st as a bombardier when I was halfway through my missions. I was shot down on Sept.5, 1944. His first mission was to the same place, Ludwigshaven, on Sept. 9, 1944. The Group also flew a mission to Ludwigshaven on Sept. 8th. The Group lost one ship on each of those three days. On the 5th we lost "My Baby", my ship. On the 8th, they lost "The Roxy Special," and on the 9th, they lost "Strickly G.I." "My Baby" and "Roxy" were from the 322 sqdn., and "Strickly G.I." was from the 323rd. Three ships and crews in three days. Pretty rough. "My Baby," lost on Sept. 5th, my plane, was the 170th B-17 and crew lost by the 91st. "The Roxy Special" lost on the Sept. 8th mission that Sam will tell you about, here, was the

171st plane lost, and "Strickly G.I." on September 9th was the 172nd, from a total, so far, of 228 missions. More than 170 B-17s, plus a couple of dozen more in accidents, etc. Nearly 2000 crewman, and thousands of families, back in the United States, (the "Zone of the Interior") seldom knowing for sure what had happened to that fine young man who had sent, in his letters, so vigorous a description of his life; and training, and then, all of a sudden, had disappeared forever to his family. Fortunately a portion of those shot down were saved by their parachutes, barbarously imprisoned, and eventually returned home, emaciated and worn in a way from which many of them never recovered. I'll tell you something about that a little latter, too, but let me get back to that. First, a message that Sam sent to all of us in the 91st computer group recently—certainly worthy of being included in this record. He wrote:

"A day in the life of the 324th squadron, 91st Group. Ludwigshaven, September 8, 1944."

"My first mission was to Ludwigshaven on September 9th, 1944. On the previous day the 324th, my squadron, had sent twelve crews to the same target. It was not one of those missions with disastrous losses of men and aircraft. We had our share of those tragedies, (Schweinfurt, Aug. 17, 1943, mission #65, eleven 91st planes lost, and Meresburg, Nov. 2, 1944, thirteen 91st planes lost), and there were other, similarly disastrous days, but this record is of the 171st mission, on September 8th, 1944, a fairly typical mission, if there can be such a thing.

The heroics recorded here were everyday actions of the men and B-17s of the 91st. Judge for yourselves the lives we lived and the memories we retain." As a matter of record, the 91st, our Group, lost more crews and B-17s than any other group in the entire Air Force. The intent of this anecdotal report is to call attention to, and to honor the courage and fortitude of the men, hardly out of boyhood, on this mission. It is in no sense a complete report. That may be compiled another day.

This mission was led by Captain Manny Klette, that most remarkable man who flew more than ninety combat missions, first with another group, and then with the 91st, --and survived. A modern day miracle. The law of averages says that that was an impossibility, but he did it---and survived.

The men who flew—and what they did on that mission:

Lt. Freemen Beasley—pilot. Flak wound through the skull. Remained conscious and gave instructions over the interphone. He dragged himself back into the pilot's seat halfway back across the channel and flew the ship with one arm paralyzed until he became sick at his stomach and had to leave his seat.

Lt. Howard Donahue—co-pilot. Did an exceptionally fine job of flying the flak-riddled aircraft where Lt. Beasley was lying wounded. At one point, with the controls jammed by the wounded pilot's body, he narrowly averted a collision, through his flying skill.

T/Sgt. Evan Zilmer—top turret gunner. Rendered skillful emergency first aid to wounded Lt. Beasley and assisted co-pilot Donahue in flying the damaged aircraft.

Lt. Gordon Lowe—Mickey navigator. Painfully wounded by flak on the bomb run. Stayed at his post until "bombs away."

Llt. Arnold O'Toole—pilot. Flak bursts smashed through the center of his foot—breaking several bones. The same burst severed some of the aircraft controls. Lt. O'Toole refused to leave his seat or relinquish control of the aircraft until the ship was out of danger. He dragged himself back to his seat as the ship neared Bassingbourn and assisted in the landing.

Lt. Elbert H. Weeks—pilot. On the bomb run his co-pilot was killed and he was painfully wounded, yet he flew the ship without mentioning his wounds (broken right hand with severed arteries and a wound in his thigh)) until the dead co pilot was taken care of. He then allowed a tourniquet to be applied to his arm and landed the ship on an airstrip in France, avoiding bomb craters and a bulldozer on the runway. Weak from loss of blood, he had to be lifted from the plane. The aircraft was so severely damaged that it was salvaged.

S/Sgt. Henry Saunders—top turret gunner (and engineer). With great skill and presence of mind, he removed the co-pilot's body from his seat, gave the pilot first aid and assisted in flying the badly damaged aircraft on the return flight.

This is not a complete report. There were many deeds of valor that day as there were on many days in the life of the 91st. These are just the men listed on one report. "A day in the life of the 324th squadron of the 91st Bomb Group." And remember, these are planes and crews that survived, that returned to fly another day. There is no way to know or to relate the bloody horror, the stress, and the agony of those who did not survive, and did not return. And there were 207 of those planes, and more than 2000 men in the crews, who did not return. A part of the hearts of those of us who survived will always remain with them. Remember, this was only one Group, the 91st. There were many more Groups of B-17s, B-24s, etc. who had similar or greater losses. Many, many thousands of the best young men our nation could produce, who disappeared from the subsequent life of their families and our nation. This war had to be fought, but all wars are disasters, and this was the greatest in history. As Tom Brokaw has said, this, indeed, was the "Greatest Generation".

Now back to Anderson, again. Remember, the 91st lost 207 planes and crews in direct combat. Many of those lost planes blew up in one explosion when hit with flak or by a fighter in a mortal spot, but most of them struggled to survive, and were destroyed only after a tremendous struggle, similar to, but less successful than those described above. That total of 207 B-17s lost, destroyed, however, means that there were 207 tragic stories, stories that we know nothing of, because those crews did not return. That's more than 2000 men, most of whom died terrible deaths, a few who survived to live in prison camps and return home after the war, many injured beyond repair. Those are men whom we should honor and revere as long as the memory of that tragic war and the heroic men who fought it continues to exist.

I'll also share with you a more pleasant record two navigators made of their trip over the cold, grey Atlantic to their new home at Bassingbourn.

The first was made in late 1943, Dec. 17th, arriving just after a period of heavy loss for the 91st. Five B-17s had been lost on the Dec. 1st mission to Leverkusen, and eight more would be lost before another month had passed. Those ships were continually being replaced by those flown in by crews such as the one described in the story below, written by its navigator, and posted on the 91st web site.

John wrote:

From my wartime diary
Gander Lake, Newfoundland
Dec. 17, 1943

"Jim (Jim Tyson, Pilot) got out of the hospital two days ago and we are ready to go. Finally it has stopped snowing and the snowplows have been working hard, trying to get the runways clear for takeoff. About noontime we were told to be ready for briefing at 2100 hours. Therefore we spent the afternoon shopping at the PX, buying what we thought we might need, paying our bills, etc.

The briefing room was crowded with the 36 crews of the Chambers Provisional Group who were scheduled to take off. According to Metro, the weather was supposed to be fairly good with 30 to 40 MPH tail winds helping us all the way. However, metro alerted us to a front we were supposed to pass through about 100 miles west of the Irish coast. I filled out my flight plan, drew in the route on my Mercator projection chart, grabbed the rest of my gear and headed for the plane that was being pre-flighted by the crew.

The gross weight of the B-17 was 58,000 lbs. We had a pretty good load aboard. Each member of the crew had a bedroll, a B4 bag, and an A3 bag tucked in the bomb bay. In addition, my Navigator's foot locker was jammed into the small nose compartment. Only the navigator knew that it didn't contain those many volumes of navigation books covering every range of latitude from the North Pole to the South. Instead, my HO-218 volumes were limited to the latitude range we would be flying. The rest of the weight and space was used up by soap, perfume, silk stocking and other "wampum" items I thought might be needed in England.

We were scheduled to take off in No. 3 position at 0000 (midnight). The fuel tanks, (main and Tokyo) were filled again after the engines were warmed up. Fuel capacity was 2750 gallons. Oil tanks were full with 36 gallons each. The # 2 plane wasn't ready to go, so we taxied down to take off position in his place. It was very cold, and the snow was piled high on each side of the runway, but the plows had done a good job of clearing the runways. The brakes were cold, and Jim had a little trouble with them sticking.

I was wearing my electric suit and regular wool pants. I wore my fleece lined flying boots over the electric boots. I wasn't nervous.

Everyone on the crew realized our chances were zero if we were forced down in the Atlantic or became lost on the way across. I surely didn't feel cocky. Nevertheless, I had every confidence in my ability to navigate the ship and crew safely across the ocean. As a final check on the newly issued octant, I ran a Ho-Hc check on it the previous day. Everything checked out fine. Jim seemed to have confidence in my navigating ability and I certainly respected him as a pilot. We were ready to go. However, if we could have foreseen what was waiting for us out over the Atlantic, I am sure we would have preferred to wait for more favorable conditions.

Dec. 18, 1943

The all clear for take off was received from the tower at 0010 hours. Just as Jim was running up the engines, a large trailer truck full of gasoline turned around in a runway intersection ahead of us. The words were hot and heavy as Bill Doherty told the tower what to do with that fuel truck. Finally, at 0021, Jim eased the throttles forward, and we started for England.

With snow piled high on each side of the runway, it seemed like we were taking off from the bottom of the Grand Canyon. The air was cold and dense and the runway was about 7000 ft. long. After two or three bounces we were airborne about ¾ of the way down the runway. Later, Sgt. Jensen said the takeoff reminded him of a big, old goose, flapping its wings and running while trying to take off from a lake. We made a wide sweeping turn and passed the airport climbing on course at 0028. We had never flown our ship at night and we discovered that my navigator's light reflected into the pilot's eyes. I stuffed my leather flight jacket up under the rudder pedals and remedied the situation.

My chart was a small scale Mercator covering the entire distance between Gander Lake and our objective, Prestwick, Scotland. We flew a great circle course because of the shorter distance and more favorable wind metro claimed we would have to comparison with a rhumb line course. The stars were bright. VERY BRIGHT ! I took my first 3 star fix about one hour after takeoff and got a ground speed of 174 knots. I had intended to use Polaris, the North Star, to determine our latitude. But we had problems. The night was so very clear, third and fourth magnitude stars looked like first and second magnitude stars. The field of view for identifying stars in the octant was quite limited. I could not positively identify Polaris, a second magnitude star, in the midst of a background of unbelievably bright third and fourth magnitude stars. Plans for using the North Star for latitude shots were abandoned. I used other, more readily identifiable stars such as Betelgeux, Sirius, Capella, Riget, and Dubhe as well as the moon.

The concern of the crew about our position was obvious. The radio operator tuned in on a station that provided accurate time checks for celestial navigators. Sgt. Churchill volunteered his services in the nose of the ship to help the navigator. I handed him the chronometer and told him to watch the second hand, and notify me immediately if it stopped. Churchill did his job well and I was relieved of the responsibility of conducting a training school when I was somewhat apprehensive, myself.

The outside temperature was a modest -10C (+4F). My three star fixes were falling in place. The first part of the trip was more or less uneventful. I obtained position reports from celestial fixes at 0228, 0328, 0436, and a final fix at 0536. The ground speeds were 197, 196, 201, and 205 respectively. (phenomenal for a B-17). We were being pushed along by a strong tailwind just a few degrees off the tail. I was getting ready to take some more star shots about 0620 when the pilot called. He told me to put my oxygen mask on as he was climbing to get over some clouds. Churchill went back to the radio room. By the time we got things rearranged in the nose of the ship and my mask in place, it had closed in all around us. This was the front the meteorologists had told us to expect. We still had about 800 miles to go. I put the octant away and kept track of our course by dead reckoning.

We were homing by radio compass on a strong radio beam at Dernyacross, Ireland, and expected to fly out of the front within 30 minutes to an hour. The temperature was -20 Deg C and we were flying smoothly at 16,700 ft. My ETA to Dernyacross was 0841. About 40 minutes out of Dernyacross the radio compass started to swing violently and had to be disregarded. We knew the storm was affecting the signal. We flew out my ETA still confident that we would clear the front as metro said we would.

Jim decided to go down and take a look below. We dropped to about 12,000 ft. and hit some very bad icing conditions. One minute the black perforated outer barrel of the machine gun sticking out the starboard navigator's window was merely a shadow in the dim light. The next minute it looked like a huge white war club. Ominously, the air speed indicator dropped to zero because the heater in the pitot tube had failed. Jim applied power, climbing to try and find an altitude where icing conditions weren't so severe. He flew by power settings from that point on. For the navigator there were no stars, radio signals or power settings to turn to. All I could use was my last three star fix position, already 2 ½ hours ancient. The wind was stronger than any I had ever observed from my navigator's table. I used this to plot our position by dead reckoning. The engines groaned as we climbed on our course to Prestwick. We finally broke out on top at 26,500 feet. Radio reception was very poor. The air was full of static, and it was cold, -50 deg F. My ETA to Prestwick was 0927. After we flew it out, I put the pilot on a corrected circle course so the wind wouldn't blow us out of the country. There was nothing else to be done. I sat quietly and listened to the radio as Jim tried to contact the Prestwick tower.

Jim could make contact with both Nutts Corner and Prestwick, but they wouldn't respond when he asked for a QDM (magnetic heading) to their base. Finally, after trying fruitlessly for about thirty minutes, he made another call to Burton (the code name for Prestwick) saying:

"Hello, Burton, this is Harry How (our code name). Come in. please." The response was loud and clear, in a cockney accent, "Ello, Airy OW, where are you?"

Jim replied, "We don't know. What is the ceiling over your base?"

The cockney accent came back, again, saying, "Ello, Airy Ow. Where are you?"

Jim replied, "We still don't know. What is the ceiling over your base?"

Once more, Prestwick came in with "Ello, Airy Ow. Where are you?"

Finally, Jim replied, "Burton, this is Harry How. We don't know where we are. We're sitting up here at 26,500 feet above a solid cloud layer in the vicinity of your field. We are low on oxygen, and running low on fuel. Our air speed indicator isn't working, and we are losing number four engine (low oil pressure). Unless you can give us some help in the next thirty minutes we are going to bail out and leave this SOB sitting up here."

The response was immediate.

"Ello, Airy Ow. Don't do that !! Fly 180 degrees and give us a long count."

Jim went through the ritual of counting slowly up to ten and back to one, again. About one minute later the tower operator came back, saying, "Fly 270 degrees and give us another long count."

Just a few seconds later he was back on the air, with "Come on down, Airy Ow, you are right over the base."

At that moment the happiest navigator in the entire 8th Air Force was sitting in the nose compartment of a B-17 numbered 237986.

Despite several queries by Jim, the tower operator had never given us the altitude of the cloud layer above the field. We were all "goosey" about going through the same bad icing conditions that we had encountered earlier.

Finally, after descending through 10,000 feet of solid clouds (without icing) we broke into clear air at 16,000 feet. We marveled at the beauty of the English countryside spread out below us. The temperature soon rose above freezing (32 deg. F) and the ice melted on the pitot tube. The air speed indicator started working again and our spirits soared.

Prestwick was a fantastic contrast to Gander Lake. Gone were the piles of snow and the snowplows. Everything was green, lush dark green and damp with moisture. It looked much like New England in late spring except the trees were bare of leaves. Dozens of aircraft were scattered about the airfield, everything from Typhoons to an old Gypsy Moth trainer biplane that looked at least 20 years old.

We grabbed our bags and started for our quarters, but we couldn't get into our rooms till after supper. I sat down in an easy chair in the lobby of the BOQ and promptly fell sound asleep. I was pooped ! About four hours later I became aware that someone was moving my legs. I awakened to find a scrubwoman on her hands and knees lifting each leg gently while she scrubbed the floor. I was quite flabbergasted, since I had never before seen a scrub person in any establishment get closer to the floor than the end of a mop handle. It was dinnertime, and I was famished. After eating, we went upstairs to our rooms, wrote a few letters home. I went to bed early to try to make up for lost sleep."

That's the way I recorded it in my diary. What I didn't record were the cuss words I let out about a month later when Jim Tyson told me he wasn't at all worried about our position. He knew that I had hit Dernyacross right on the button because the marker beacon indicator on his panel lit up right about the time of my ETA. But the son of a gun never told me about it, and I desperately needed that check point at that time.".

John Howland brought his plane in, flew his missions in the 324th sqdn. and survived to return to the "Zone of the Interior."

Another navigator, George Jacobs, read John Howland's story of his trip over, and summarized his own story. And I'm repeating these stories because they are typical of what so many young men of the America of those days did. They learned skills which were undreamed of two years before, used those skills to help destroy the "evil axis" which was threatening to engulf our Western Civilization and returned home to create new lives for themselves in the America which had been fashioned by their actions, their incredible bravery, their unbelievable ability to learn and to do, and their strength of character to remain true to their mission and their purpose. They were a part of that incredible combat Group that flew 340 combat missions, beginning on November 7th, 1942, to the sub pens at Brest, and closing with that violently wild mission to Pilsen on April 25, 1945, on which, incredibly, there were no casualties.

The 91st was the first Group to complete 100 missions, to Tours, on May 1, 1944. They had the most enemy aircraft destroyed in combat, 420. Most important, overriding all----many hundreds of them, all volunteers, gave their lives so that we could have the world we have, today. And there were many more Groups like them, as brave, as skilled, as heroic, as memorable. I only cite the 91st because

I knew them so well----I was a part of it. I was so fortunate. I lived, while so many others did not.

Now to the story of the other navigator, George Jacobs, who navigated a similar flight, a year later.

George, in a story written as a companion to John's, said,

"John, I flew the Atlantic for the first time almost a year later than you, less than six months after my 20th birthday. We picked up a brand new B-17 at Hunter Field, Georgia. The first stop on our way to Prestwick was Fort Dix, New Jersey. I was flying with a crew that I had occasionally flown with during final training. Our flight was to take us next to Grenier Field at Manchester, N.H., but the pilot noted that the route passed almost directly over his home, which I recall was North Adams, Mass. I also noted that it went directly over my hometown of Brooklyn. The pilot said, "George, let's keep this to ourselves. I intend to buzz N. Adams as a goodbye gesture." I reluctantly said "O.K.," then pointed out that we were going to pass right over my house in Brooklyn. He said, "O.K., it's a deal. We'll go down and wave goodbye to your house, as well." And that we did.

Next stop was Gander, Newfoundland. Like you, we encountered mountains of snow packed along the sides of the runway. Because of bad weather we enjoyed a respite of a day or two before heading across the Atlantic. We also left at night. Almost from the time of reaching flight altitude we had a thick undercast below us. Unlike your case, almost everyone went to sleep on the plane, and I was left pretty much alone "downstairs." I could do no visual navigation, and even if I could there would not be much to see but water ! I took my octant out of its wooden box and started shooting star fixes. Having plenty of time to myself I shot mostly 3 star fixes, but at times I went up to five. They fell nicely in place so that I had a good track, and was able to calculate windage. I was able to locate Polaris quite well, and this let me check latitude lines between the star fixes. I also used the radio DF stations from Bluie West in southern Greenland and from Keplific, Iceland, to get some confirming LOPs. Everyone was asleep but the co-pilot and me. I guess they had a lot of confidence in me, and, as you, I had confidence in myself ! The star fixes, Polaris sightings and, shortly after the sun rose, a nice sun shot gave me a confirmed longitude check. About that time the pilot asked me for a bearing and ETA for our landfall position. This was a bit critical because we had to avoid flying over the Republic of Ireland, which was neutral during the War. I gave him the bearing and ETA for the entrance to Donegal Bay, which was the designated route to Northern Ireland, and then on to Scotland.

The pilot started to lose altitude through the undercast that we had encountered for the entire trip. Suddenly, there to our right, I could see the northwestern tip of the Irish Republic. We were right on course for the center of Donegal Bay. The intercom barked and the pilot shouted, "Jacobs, you are a half-assed Navigator. You missed your ETA by 25 seconds, and you missed your landfall by about a halfmile." I gave him the final bearing to Prestwick, but I think that he flew the beacons there. Like you, I have an indelible picture in my mind of that lush, green terrain of Northern Ireland and then Scotland, below us."

Howland and Jacobs both completed their tours, returned to the "Zone Of The Interior," and remain a part of the "91st" Association, today.

Pilots, navigators, bombardiers, engineers and gunners who flew we read much about, and rightly so, because so many of them died serving their country and their fellows in that bloody war. But those who served on the ground, with no chance to earn a trip home, should be recognized, too, for what they did. Without their fortitude, their skills, and their incredible ingenuity, the flying crews could have never have done what they did. A man named Whit Hill, who was a member of the engineering and sheet-metal crew, shared his story with us, recently, and I'll share it with you.

He said, "All through the months and years of combat, battle damage to our bombers which survived to return from their combat missions was extraordinary, and those planes were always needed back on the flight line for the next mission. As a result we were always pushed to get those ships back on flying status. The word was, "how soon," and the response better be "tomorrow morning, or at least damn soon."

"After one mission a 323rd squadron B-17 (OR) received what appeared to be a few flak hits which could be rapidly repaired. One hit in the #2 engine nacelle didn't appear to be too serious. However, on a closer look, there was damage to one of the four brackets used to attach the number two engine to the wing, damage which would require major work. The Squadron engineering officer came up with the usual "how soon" question. There were no spare engine mount brackets available. Our 323rd squadron sheet metal crew was on the spot. We studied the damage and pointed out that we could duplicate the bracket if we had the right annealed aluminum sheet metal of the same thickness (.052 or .064 thousandths) as the damaged bracket. It would, of course, be necessary to heat treat and harden the annealed new bracket after it was formed. Hardened thick aluminum usually cracks when bent sharply. Heat treating the soft annealed bracket could be accomplished in the base central heating furnaces that provided hot water heat to the barracks and buildings. It was a "fix it or let the plane sit" situation. Let it sit ? No self respecting sheet metal crew would allow that. The squadrons were assigned nine B-17s each. No spares. It was a hard time. Losses were mounting. The Group needed every ship that could fly. Our option was to try making the bracket to get the plane back on flying status, or watch it sit until a part was located back in the States and shipped to us. In addition, the danger existed that if we let it sit, a crew from another squadron, desperate for parts, as we were, would sneak in and cannibalize the ship to provide parts for their own damaged planes. After discussing the problem with the engineering officer, with us suggesting that we might be able to create the bracket, ourselves, Harold (Bumps) Elliot and I were told to use our ingenuity to create the bracket and re-attach the engine—and do it NOW. The plane was needed tomorrow. Sooo—we carefully removed the damaged engine mount bracket, then, using the soft annealed aluminum sheet metal supplied by the RAF maintenance people who were still on the base, we made two models, and checked them for fit. Then we went to the base central heating plant, where we coated the brackets and test strips with yellow lye soap—"Grandmother's lye soap." We were amazed, when we tested, how hard the metal became, and how the strips would "sing" when struck. Finally we placed the soaped-up bracket on one of the long coal shovels, eased it into a hot furnace, and cautiously watched the lye soap color. In time the soap coating turned brown. Quickly we removed the shovel and bracket from the furnace and let them cool on the floor. When cool, we washed off the soap, then fitted the bracket onto the engine mount, scribed the rivet holes, center punched and drilled out the holes, fitted the bracket in place, inserted and bucked the rivets, and 'walla', the job was finished. We knew that when hardening iron or steel, the material is generally heated to cherry red, and then immersed into cold water or oil. Heat treating aluminum is just the opposite. Cooling the aluminum slowly hardens it, while quenching it in cool water softens it. The job done, Carl Proctor, the Crew Chief, taxied the plane from the hanger to the Wimpole Hall dispersal area, and made ready for the next day's mission. We, the crew chief and I, kept tabs on the status of the bracket after each subsequent mission. No cracks or failures were ever observed. The plane was eventually shot down and we lost track of our bracket creation, but our long night's work kept the squadron at full strength for the next day's mission." (Please note the statement, "The plane was eventually shot down")

This was possible because Bassingbourn had a central heating plant, duplicated on no other American air base. Because of this, and similar luxuries, Bassingbourn was called the "Country Club." Most American bases, and some English, were usually ankle deep in mud. The staff lived in Quonset huts heated by coal stoves and hot water was practically non-existent. It was a difficult existence. We at Bassingbourn knew how lucky we were because we constantly heard stories of the physical miseries suffered by our friends at other bases. And we were fortunate in other ways. We were near Cambridge, where quite a large group of young women, who worked in various war industries, were quartered. This made for a great deal of 'companionship', but also a great deal of heartbreak. By the close of combat the 91st had lost 207 B-17s in combat, and many, many men who were so seriously injured (but returned) that they did not survive. Keep in mind that this was just one Group. There were 41 Heavy Bombardment Groups and 19 fighter Groups in the 8th Air Force. If the losses in the 91st were typical, and they were, that means that in Heavy Bombers alone more than 40,000 men were lost. What a tragic, heroic waste of our finest resource, and what an argument for avoiding such future disastrous ventures---wherever possible.

Some of the most gripping of the memories of the 91st have been researched and written by a historian, Lowell Getz, who with his researching of our history has almost become a part of the 91st. The book he was written, "Mary Ruth" Memories of Mobile' contains some of the most graphic and well written of our memories. He tells the story of the 91st's part in the mission to Wilhelmshaven on May 21, 1943, during which we lost four planes, ORX, (no name) from the 322nd sqdn., and "Desperate Journey", DJF, and Marie Jane from the 324th sqdn.

The stories I've shared with you, here, are those that I have a personal awareness of. They happened. To men from my Group.

Let me include one more story. One that was told to me by a member of our 91st Group, but one which I cannot personally vouch for. Anyway, as it was told to me by a member of our Group. He said:

"Stories we've been sharing of evadees remind me of a story that I heard at the American bar at the "Potomac", pronounced by the Brits as the "Pot-o-mac" with emphasis on the first syllable. I took a seat at the bar and ordered a pint of "bitter". There was only one other person in the bar. He was an American officer in class A uniform who was also having a "pint". We looked at each other and I said, "I think I know you." He said, "I thought you looked familiar to me, too." Striking up a conversation with someone you didn't know, in London at that time, was discouraged, but we thought we knew each other, and after some friendly conversation we figured it out. We were both pilots in the 91st and, like myself, he had spent a lot of time in the Combat Mess playing snooker, ping-pong, BS ing, and guzzling beer. I said to him, "I haven't seen you in quite a while. Where have you been ?" There being no other person around, including the bartender, he told me the following story. I have no reason to believe it was anything but the truth.

He was shot down—this would have been late 1943—over France. He was the only survivor, but he was picked up and hidden as he reached the ground. His rescuers had a connection with the underground so he was given some civilian clothes and whisked away to a large house near a German airfield, and hidden in the attic. He soon realized that the house was a house of prostitution serving the

Luftwaffe personel stationed nearby. I recalled a briefing from an RAF instructor at Bovingdon, in 1943, during which he told about how the Luftwaffe pilots, like the RAF and the Americans, took nothing with them on a flight except their "dog tags". But there was one exception. No respectable Luftwaffe pilot would leave behind his "nookie" ration card. Somehow or other the RAF got hold of a list of all the prostitution houses and their locations. When a German pilot was captured, his base and unit could be identified by his ration card.

So here was this American pilot sitting next to me telling me he had been 'housed' in such a "house." He had my immediate attention. From the small attic window he could look out at the airfield. If I remember correctly, it was an FW-190 fighter outfit. The aircraft were parked around the perimeter of the field for dispersal. The field, itself, was surrounded by a high fence, but not so high that he couldn't get over it. He watched the pattern of the guards, and, after figuring out a safe time, he slipped out of the house, climbed the fence, and actually got into the cockpit of an FW. In the dark he tried to figure out what each control was, and how he might be able to get the engine started, take off, and fly the plane back to England. He said he did this exercise more than once, but there was one thing in the cockpit he couldn't figure out. Now this is his story, as I remember it, so if there's an error here I didn't catch it, but this is the way he told it. The "thing" he couldn't figure out was a funnel shaped object located below the center of the instrument panel, and forward of the control stick. It looked like a relief tube. He wasn't sure of it. Since he couldn't be quite sure what it was, and what it was used for, he abandoned his thought of escaping by starting the plane and flying it back to England. He said he later found out it was an engine priming cup. Fuel was poured into the cup and then hand-pumped into the engine cylinder to start the engine. Kind of primitive, what? So, reluctantly, he abandoned the attempt. After a couple of months in 'confinement' the Underground arranged for him to be moved to another location—another house some miles to the south. With this move, and one or two more, he gradually worked his way toward the Pyranees, and then was able to make a try for Spain. He made it, and was eventually repatriated to England. We finished our beer, parted, and I never saw him, again. He is, to the best of my knowledge, the only American pilot who was ever saved by the beneficence of a House or Houses of prostitution."

Another story, from another Group, is so fascinating that I will include it here. It happened, although I was not there to see it. And it is proof that even in the horror of war, some miraculous, good things do happen.

One of the most miraculous of those things occurred on the October 8, 1943, mission to Bremen. It was a difficult mission. The 91st lost one plane, OR-S from the 323rd, but what happened to a part of the crew of plane # 75 (no name) in our companion Group, the 381st, that day, defies belief. # 75 took over as deputy lead in the 381st when that deputy lead went down. # 75 had already lost an engine and she lost another when German fighters hit her. With two engines gone she was forced to drop back to another Group, and then to another. Finally they were alone and the ferocity of the attacks increased, so that the pilot interphoned, "Prepare to bail out, but don't go, yet." One of the waist gunners called, "Oxygen out on the co-pilot side" and they switched to the other side. The ball turret gunner interphoned to the pilot that gas was leaking from the # 2 engine over the bottom of the ship, and that firing his guns could set the ship on fire, then he climbed out of the turret. Twenty minutes after dropping their bombs, out of ammunition and badly damaged, the front of the nose was knocked off, either by an overhead attack or by a loose propeller from the windmilling # 3 engine. The pilot called, "bail out." The navigator and one of the waist gunners were able to get out of the ship through the forward hatch. The tail gunner was able to get to the other waist gunner, who was injured. When the nose blew off the plane went into a dive, then broke in half at the waist. The tail gunner and the waist gunner were trapped in the aft section of the plane, with no way out. Berk, the injured waist gunner, lost consciousness, and McCook, the tail gunner, could only hang onto Berk and the tail section, as it floated, upright, to the ground. Incredibly, both survived, with minor injuries. McCook was able to leave the tail, but was captured immediately by the Germans. When the Germans checked in the open tail section they found Berk, unconscious, with a battered jaw and injured arm and leg, but in good shape, otherwise. This after a many thousand foot fall in a broken-off, open tail section. Berk was transported to a German hospital, given adequate care, later repatriated to the United States in a prisoner-of-war exchange, and after the war worked as a crash investigator for the Federal Aviation Agency. McCook remained in a prison camp until the end of the war, then re-enlisted in the Air Force, spent time in Korea, and eventually retired.

Free fall from twenty thousand feet in a broken-off tail section, and they both survived. Yes, there were some miracles.

One of those was simply the survival of a crew from the 326th sqdn. of the 92nd Group on the Hanover raid on July 17, 1943, Lieutenant Robert Campbell, pilot. -----This is one of the very few stories that I will include that is not of the 91st, but since it is so well reported in General McLaughlin's book, "The Mighty 8th In WW II," and parallels several stories of the 91st, I thought the 92nd should be represented in my work, however briefly.

On this mission, as the 92nd formation approached the coast, the plane flown by Lt. Campbell was singled out for attack by a group of FW 190s. On their first pass, the navigator, Lt. Keith Koske, knew they had been hit. There was a terrific explosion overhead. In a few seconds the top turret gunner and engineer, S. Sgt. Tyre Weaver, fell from his turret and slumped to the floor at the rear of the nose compartment. When Lt. Koske got to him he saw that his left arm had been blown off at the shoulder and he was a mass of blood. Koske tried to inject some morphine, but the needle had been bent and he couldn't get it to go in. However it was best that he not be given the morphine. The first thing was to try to stop the loss of blood. They tried to apply a tourniquet, but it proved impossible, as the arm was off too close to the shoulder. They knew he had to have medical treatment as soon as possible, and they had almost four hours flying time in front of them, so there was no alternative. Koske opened the escape hatch, adjusted Weaver's chute and placed the ripcord ring firmly in his right hand. Weaver became excited, pulled the ripcord and the pilot chute opened in the updraft. Koske gathered it together, tucked it under his right arm, set him in a crouched position with his legs through the hatch, made certain that his good arm was holding the chute folds tight against his body, and toppled him out into space.

Koske then called down to the ball turret gunner, Sgt. James Ford, and asked him to observe. Ford said that the chute opened O.K. They were at 25,000 feet, twenty five miles due west of Hanover. Their hope was that he would be seen descending, picked up, and given medical attention immediately.

The bombardier, Lt. Asa Irwin, had been busy with the nose guns. He fought off the attacking FW 190s, dropped his bombs with the Group, and came back to his nose guns. However the attacks were now all coming from the tail. Koske tried to use his interphone several times, but could get no answer. The last he remembered hearing over it was shortly after the first attack, when someone was complaining about not getting any oxygen. Except for what felt like occasional violent evasive action the plane seemed to be flying O.K. About two hours later, when they were about fifteen minutes out from the enemy coast, Lt. Koske decided to go up, check with the pilot, whom he couldn't raise on the intercom, and have a look around. He found the pilot, Lt. Campbell, slumped down in his seat, a mass of blood, with the back of his head blown off. This had happened about two hours before, at the first attack. A shell had entered from the right side, crossed in front of Flt. Officer John Morgan, co-pilot, and hit Lt Campbell in the back of the head. Morgan was flying the plane with one hand, holding the half-dead pilot with the other hand, and he had been doing it for more than two hours. Morgan told Koske that they had to get Campbell out of his seat so he could get in it to land the ship. the glass on the co-pilot's side, where the shell entered, was so badly shattered that he could not see out to land the ship—if they made it back. Koske and Morgan struggled for what seemed an eternity to get Campbell out of his seat and down into the rear of the navigator's compartment, where the bombardier held him from slipping out the open hatch. Morgan was operating the controls with one hand, trying to help Koske with Campbell with the other, and keeping the plane, roughly, in the 92nd formation. When Morgan asked why Koske had not received help from the other crewmen, Koske told him that the crewmen in the rear were unconscious or on the edge of unconsciousness from lack of oxygen, the oxygen lines having been shattered in the first attack, several hours before. The ship had been undefended, except for the nose and ball turret guns. Flight Officer Morgan's feat had been little short of miraculous. He had kept the ship in formation and, holding the fatally wounded pilot off the controls with one hand, had flown to and from the target alone, unaided, with no radio, no interphone, and no hydraulic fluid. And he brought that ship safely home to an emergency landing on an emergency field near the British coast. In early December, 1943, the War Department awarded now 2nd Lieutenant Morgan the Congressional Medal of Honor. It was later learned that S/Sgt. Tyre Weaver had been picked up by the Germans, hospitalized, was recovering, and was later repatriated to his home in Alabama.

Yes, there were miracles. War is a combination of Hell and miracles, but there were not enough miracles to go around, and it would have taken more miracles than were available, as the war wound down, to ease the heartbreak that occurred as the more than sixty combat bases maintained by the American forces in England began to close. Many of the airmen and more of the ground services (some of whom had been there three or more years) had formed strong attachments. Some war brides were brought home, but many were not and a string of heartbreak reached across England, over Europe and back through the United States as liaisons were formed and dissolved, voluntarily or involuntarily, too often ending in misery for both parties. And if there was heartbreak in England, there was much more back in our homeland. The thousands of men lost from the 8th Air Force and other units all left sweethearts and/or families back home, many of whom never knew what happened to their loved ones

After earnings my wings and graduating from 'advanced', when I flew back to Salt Lake City (Fort Douglas) to be assigned to a combat crew, then go to Louisiana for combat training I passed a stewardess quietly crying in the stewardess' back seat section. I sat down beside her and asked if I could help. She couldn't stop the tears, but she told me she'd just called home (Pasadena) and been told that her fiance's family had received a telegram saying that he had been killed in action—he was a bombardier on a B-17 crew in England. I had a free week in Salt Lake City before I was assigned to a crew and shipped to Louisiana, so I spent much of it with her, trying to comfort her. She wrote to me during my combat training and combat days and the pictures she sent me were tantalizing. When I left the service to enter college, I stayed with her family for a few days while looking for a place to live near UCLA. Fraternities pressed me, but I'd lived with groups of men for three years and I'd had enough of that. She pressed for marriage, and oh, I would have liked to, but the only skill I possessed was flying, and I needed a respite from that, so the only way I could have supported a family was to work in her father's photography shop, and I didn't think that was fair to either of us, so as my months in college lengthened, we drifted apart, and I finally received an invitation to her wedding. My aching heart kept me away, and I never saw her again.

At UCLA I did four years in three, then a year of graduate work, including a teaching credential. I lived on the GI Bill, some construction work, and a minimum of pay from the Air Force reserve for an occasional flight, including one summer of training at Tucson, where I put in some time in B-29s. Those things could fly forever, with a minimum of effort from the pilot, but I didn't like them much. I guess I still had a sentimental attachment to that gutty, marvelous B-17—unpressurised and noisy, but full of heart, character, and memories.

A classmate, whose father was a part of the court retinue of the Shah of Iran, offered to buy me a plane if I would fly him home for a visit. I was tempted, but I was concerned that once in I might have trouble getting out, and I still had a life to live. So I stopped in at the placement office at UCLA one day. The superintendent from Redlands was there looking for a junior high school teacher. Redlands, seventy miles east of Los Angeles, an orange grove community, sounded good to me, so I took the job and began a new life—again. That life included the most beautiful blue-eyed blonde that I'd ever seen, teaching art down the hall from me. I persuaded her to marry me and we began a new series of adventures, including being chased, in a canoe, down the Zambezi in Zimbabwe by a very angry hippo—but that's another story.

When I left the 91st and came back from the war in Europe I went through the Air Force Central Instructors' School in San Antonio, instructed for a while in B-25s (the twin engine medium bomber that

Jimmy Doolittle used to drop the first bombs on Tokyo, but which was now being used to train cadets in Advanced Flight School) then transferred to the Ferry Command so I could fly some of the more exciting planes, which I'd never been in. I did, and flew many of them to their modification or embarkation ports, from where they would be flown to combat zones. My favorite was the P-38, a spirited twin engine, twin tailed beauty that responded to a pilot's touch as eagerly as my sorrel pony that I guided with my knees while I threw in newspapers when I was a youngster. I was in a P-38 that day in August of 1944 when I watched Richard Bong die in an experimental jet as he took off from Burbank. That decided me. I left the Air Force, got an education and began a career as a teacher, the most fascinating work in the world.

Many years later, after I'd found some of my flying group through the internet, a fine artist, John Doughty, did a lithograph of two 91st B-17s returning from a mission to Meresburg. That mission was on November 2nd, 1944. It was a deadly one. The 91st lost 13 planes that day, nearly half of the Group. The control wheel was shot out of Tom's hand, but none of the crew were wounded, another miracle. I was on my way back home, but if I'd been allowed to fly on that mission I most certainly would not have survived. The rest of my friends from those days, with the exception of Tom and our crew, were all lost. All this I learned years later, while researching this history. The plane that John lithographed, old 909, I flew in a time or two, if I remember correctly, although the mission he illustrated was flown after I had been shot down, returned and sent home, so I, with a few other veterans of the 91st that John located, gathered, and signed the lithographs for him. We understand that one of them has now been placed in the White House. We hope it is a symbol of a war that had to be fought, but must never be fought again. That lithograph, with John's permission, appears as an initial illustration in this book, so it seems almost a part of me, as this writing is.

John asked each of us who signed the lithograph to write a brief memory of the days we flew, to be included with the lithographs. We did and I'll close this set of memories with what I wrote. It includes a picture that a gunner snapped, from a side window, of the P-51 that picked us up as we were forced from our formation by the loss of an engine as we returned from a mission to destroy the docks at Kiel, my fourteenth mission. That P-51 pilot saved our lives, but we never found out who he was. If he's still alive, this is my "thank you."

I said, somewhere above, that I'd tell you another story or two of the 91st before ending this account. One of the most vivid is the record written by Lowell Getz in his book "Mary Ruth," the story of the B-17 "Eagle's Wrath." That plane, piloted by Captain Charles Glaque, flew on a mission to the docks of Wilhelmshaven on the 21st of May, 1943. The 91st was leading the strike force that day, with "Eagle's Wrath" leading the second element of the lead squadron as deputy lead for the strike force.

The Group assembled above the base at 13,000 feet, and began the climb to 22,000 feet while crossing the Channel. When approaching the German controlled coast about 50 German fighters flew out to intercept the bombers. They were driven off with little damage, but a short time later another attack, by a new 200 fighters, was a different matter. They attacked as the bombers, approaching Wilhelmshaven, turned at the I.P. (initial point of the bomb run) to begin the approach. The first wave of fighters hit the 91st lead ship, the "Careful Virgin," with Captain Wm. Clancy, pilot, and Lt. Col. Wm. Reid, the Group lead, acting as his co-pilot. A German fighter sent 20 mm fire into the "Virgin's" number four engine, setting it afire. Captain Clancy feathered the engine and continued leading the Group on its approach to the target. As "Eagle's Wrath" approached the target, a shell went through the nose, right under the arched body of the bombardier, Lt. Butler, as he bent over the bomb sight. Butler stayed at the sight. The Group dropped their bombs on the target and pulled away from the coast.

Three minutes after "bombs away" an ME 109 left a group of ten German fighters and came at "Eagle's Wrath" head on. Lt. Butler fired 150 rounds from his nose gun at the fast closing fighter, which flew to within 25 yards of "Eagle's Wrath." The fighter began spinning down with its engine and right wing on fire. From another closing fighter another shell came through "Eagle's" nose, again missing Lt. Butler by a hair. A few minutes later, as the Group was moving out over the North Sea, another ME 109 flew from 100 yards out, at 11:00 o'clock. Butler fired 100 rounds at it. It fell off to the left, with its engine smoking, and spun downward. A wing broke off, and it spun into the water. The fighters broke away as the Group moved out to sea, but the 91st had lost four ships, one from the 322, OR-X, and three from the 324th, Desperate Journey, DFJ (no name), and Marie Jane. Four ships and forty men. And worse, on the disastrous mission to Schweinfurt, on August 17th, the 91st lost eleven planes-110 men. Lt. Anthony Arcaro was the pilot on "Eagle's Wrath" that day. They started out on the left wing of Lt. Charles Bennett in "Stupentakit", who was flying lead of the second element of the low squadron. Lt. Von der Hyde, in "V-Packette" was flying right wing of the second element. While the Group was forming up, over England, "Local Girl," Robert Wine, pilot, flying number 3 in the low element, had to abort because of engine problems, leaving five planes in the low squadron. German fighters pressed their attack as the Group crossed the enemy coast. "V-Packette" went down as they crossed the Belgian border. Next "Stupentakit" went down. Lt. Arcaro moved "Eagle's Wrath" into the vacant "Stupentakit" position. Fighters continued to move in from every direction. One Me 109, flying on its back, the pilot hanging upside down in his harness, flew directly across "Eagle Wrath's" nose. It went by so fast that none of the gunners had time to fire on it. South of Frankfurt "My Prayer" flown by Lt. James Judy, dropped out, on fire. Lt. Arcaro moved "Eagle's Wrath" up into that spot. Now only the lead plane, "The Careful Virgin", Capt. Harry Lay, pilot, and "Eagle's Wrath" were left in the low squadron. Arcaro tucked his left wing up against "Careful Virgin" and hung in tight. Even with the all-out fighter attacks, the "Eagle" had not yet been hit, but a few moments later four fighters in succession hit her. The oxygen system was set afire, the navigator, Lt. Warner, was seriously wounded, and the ball turret gunner, Sgt. Michaud, was killed. The top turret gunner (the engineer) Sgt. James Jones, was hit and killed at his position as he tried to salvo the bombs to reduce the weight of the plane. Lt. Arcaro realized he could not keep "Eagle's Wrath" in the air. The intercom was shot out and that plane had no "bail-out" bell. He sent the co-pilot, Lt. Roman Niemczyk, to the rear to tell the crewmen to bail out. Sgt. Lindholm and the right waist gunner, S/Sgt. Ralph Dearth, went out the waist hatch. The tail gunner, Sgt. Wm. Golden, dropped through the tail hatch. The radio operator,

Sgt. Delmar Kaech, tried to bail out through the bomb bay, but it was completely engulfed in fire. He then wiggled out through the upper gun port in the radio compartment and rolled off, hoping he would miss the vertical and horizontal stabilizers. Miraculously, he did. Lt. Arcaro waited a couple of minutes for the crew to have time to leave the ship. The fire in the fuselage continued to intensify. Arcaro set the autopilot, snapped on his chute and dived through the raging fire from the flight deck through the open nose hatch. Lts. Niemczyk and Warner and the bombardier, Lt. Glover, also bailed out through the nose hatch. Lt. Warner's chute apparently malfunctioned. He did not survive. The flaming "Eagle's Wrath" crashed to earth a third of a mile from Worms, Germany, one of eleven planes lost from the 91st, that day.

These stories are hard for me to tell. My last mission, in "My Baby" lives in my memory, with me always wondering if one more "jink" of the ship would have saved the tail gunner who died in the hail of fire which ripped through us. Remember, the 91st lost 207 B-17s in combat, each of which, I'm sure, had a story like some I have related. Those men are gone, but their memories linger on for those of us who flew with and after them. God bless them. Tom Brokaw was right when he named them "The Greatest Generation..

After returning to the "Zone of the Interior", I went through C.I.S. (Central Instructors' School), then instructed in B-25s for a while, but that was too quiet for me, so I transferred to the 'Ferry Command' and flew some of the Air Force's most exciting ships of those days, particularly the twin tailed P-38, one of our hottest fighters, then. One day, circling above the Burbank Airport, where I had just picked up a new P-38 that I was to deliver to a modification center at Birmingham, I watched as an odd looking plane, with no propellers, took off, below. I had left Europe just before German jets began hitting our formations, so it took me a moment to realize that this was a jet, the first I had ever seen. The Air Force had brought one of our most accomplished pilots, Richard Bong, back from the Pacific War to test fly the newly developed Air Force jets. As I watched, he reached the end of the runway, lifted into the air and blew up.

I loved flying, but there was a world beyond it that I had not touched. I had applied for and received a four engine commercial pilot's license, but I had no education beyond the Air Force, so I flew on to Birmingham, ruminating. If it could happen to Bong, it could happen to me.

Two days later I picked up an A-26 (a very 'hot' twin engine bomber) at a Douglas plant. I simply don't remember where I took it, but it must have been a long trip, because my 'flight time' log for that day shows several hours of flying time. I do remember, however, that as I filed my flight plan for the trip I thought to myself that I'd do something I hadn't done, before. My ordinary refueling stop would have been Albequerque, but this time I'd do something different. There was an air strip at a little place called "Mormon Lake". Probably a training base. I didn't know. I'd never been there, but it wasn't far out of the way, and it was new country to me, so I filed a flight plan which included a stop at "Mormon Lake". But I made an almost fatal mistake. There is an information file for pilots (or there was at that time) called 'Notams', meaning notices to airmen, which lists things pilots should know about places they are planning to land. There was a 'Notam' in the file concerning "Mormon Lake", but I neglected to read it. A bad, careless mistake. As I found, later, the "Notam" said "Runway under repair". I refueled somewhere else, first, then arrived at "Mormon Lake" to refuel again and found the only runway long enough to land my A-26 on was under repair, with nearly half of it blocked off. I didn't have enough fuel left to go elsewhere--a bad moment. Pilots who make that kind of mistake often don't live long enough to repeat it, but I was fortunate. During my time in Central Instructors' School I had been taught most of what there was to know about twin engine (medium) bombers. One procedure was a "short field" landing procedure that had been developed for the B-25s which were to make the first bombing raid on Tokyo. I used that procedure, landed my A-26 on about half of the runway ordinarily required, wiped away the sweat, and went in for a coke while my plane was being refueled. There was a sailor inside who said, "Lieutenant, I've been waiting here two days to find a ride out. Would you take me with you?" That was strictly against the rules, of course, but there were two seats in my cockpit. One was empty, so I said, "Sure, come along". He climbed in. I did a "short field" take-off, missing the runway barrier by inches. I wiped away the sweat again as he turned to me and said, "Gosh, that was fun. Will you do it again at Dallas?" I dropped him off at Dallas and flew on to where-ever I was to leave the A-26.

Back to that trip to Birmingham for a moment.

That was mid-July of 1945. I don't remember ever being checked out in a P-38, but I was in one, in the air, headed for my first refueling stop, El Paso. I had been transferred, at my request, to Ferry Command Headquarters at Long Beach. I'd instructed a while in B-25s at Minter Field, in Bakersfield, but that was too quiet for me, so I wangled a transfer to the Ferry Command. As soon as I got there they gave my a re-check in B-25s, to be sure I knew what I was doing, then an instruments check to be sure my white instruments card was honest. I'd been through Central Instructors' School in San Antonio (the toughest school in the Air Force) so both my twin engine skills and instruments card were clear, so they sent me to Lockheed, to pick up a P-38 and deliver it to Birmingham. I climbed into that P-38, ran through the check list, started the engines and took off, having the time of my life. I did aerobatics all over the San Fernando Valley sky, mostly orange groves at that time, and then headed out over the desert to El Paso, which was my first refueling stop on the way to Birmingham. Halfway to El Paso I saw a coyote below, trotting along in a wash. I grew up as a sheep-man's son in Utah, and I was not fond of coyotes, so I winged over, put down the flaps and went down to give that coyote a hard time. When they checked that '38 out to me in Burbank they left the wing-tip tanks on it. I didn't have enough experience to know that was odd, and I somehow missed them on the check-list before I took off, so I took off on the little bit of gas that had been left in the wing-tip tanks and flew out over the desert. When I rolled over to go down after that coyote and got down right next to the ground, those wing-tip tanks ran out of gas. Thank God for Air Force training. I didn't have time to think, but I automatically switched to the main tanks. The engines caught, I wiped away the sweat (again) and flew on, leaving the coyote to meander on his way by himself. That was an eventful trip for my first time in a P-38. When I got to Birmingham they gave me another P-38 that needed a modification that could only be done at Burbank and sent me west with it. My first refueling stop was Dallas. No air-conditioning, of course, and the Dallas heat was almost more than I could bear, so I re-fueled in a hurry and took off. Just as I reached take-off speed the right tire blew. I didn't want to stay anyplace that hot for as long as would be needed for replacement, so I didn't land to have it replaced. I flew on to my next refueling stop, El Paso. I called in, told them that I had a bad tire, and asked them to be ready to replace it. They evidently hadn't had recent experience with tire problems, which, in this case would pull my plane off to the right, so as I came down the approach I saw a line-up of fire engines and ambulances on the right side of the runway, right where my blown tire would turn me. It's the only time I remember using nasty language over the mike. I told them to get those blankety-blank engines out of there in a hurry.. I don't remember what they did, 'cause I landed the thing on its left wheel and held it long enough that I didn't ground-loop and hit them. The major who was in the tower that day came down, said he'd never seen that done, before, and congratulated me. I didn't tell him that I'd had practice with B-17s with blown tires that were a great deal more difficult to land than a P-38. I don't remember how I got out of El Paso. I guess they replaced the tire and I flew out, but I remember being relieved once I got back to the BOQ (bachelor officers' quarters) in Long Beach that I hadn't been stranded in a hospital in Dallas or El Paso. I never had any other problem with a P-38. They were wonderful planes to fly. My log shows that I flew a number of them out of Burbank before I'd had enough and left the Air Force. I left one week, entered UCLA the next week, and began a new life. But that's another story.

BIBLIOGRAPHY

A Kriegie's Memoirs Frank Farr
Self Published Available at 'Amazon.com'

Album of Memories Tom Brokaw
Random House New York

A Real Good War Sam Halpert
Southern Heritage Press St. Petersburg, Fla.

Bomber Pilot William Wheeler
Rutledge Books Danbury, Conn.

Combat Crew John Cromer
Warner Books Little, Brown and Co.
(U.K.—London)

Destiny's Child John R. Paget
Self published Lib of Congress
Cat. Card # TXU 856-94

Dirty Little Secrets of WW II Dunnigan and
William Morrow New York Nofi

Fear No More   David McCarthy
DAM Books Pittsburg, Penn.

Greatest Generation (The)   Tom Brokaw
Random House New York

Half A Wing, Three Engines And A Prayer   Brian D. O'Neil
McGraw Hill New York

Hell In The Heavens   William Hess
Specialty Press Publishers North Branch,
Minn. 55056

"Mary Ruth" Memoirs Of Mobile—Stories From the 91st
Lowell Getz Self Published Some of the best writing of the war.

Memphis Belle (The) Menno Duerksen
Castle Books Memphis, Tennessee

Mighty Eighth (The) Roger Freeman
Castle and Co. London, England

Mighty Eighth In WW II
Brig. Gen. J. Kemp McLaughlin USAFR
(Ret.)

Plane Names and Fancy Noses   Ray Bowden
Design Oracle Partnership, London, England

Ragged Irregulars Of Bassingbourn   Havelaar and
Schiffer Publishing Atglen, Penn.   Hess

Serenade To The Big Bird Bert Stiles
Bantam Books, New York

Stormy Weather—A B-17 G.P. Birdsong
Hambleden Publishing Co. Dublin. Calif.

Story of World War II D. Miller
Simon and Schuster New York (Revised from Commager)

Their Deeds Of Valor Don Lassiter
X Libris Corp. Lib. Of Congress

USA The Hard Way Roger W. Armstrong
Quail House Publishing Co. Orange Co. Ca.

Vignettes Of A B-17 Combat Crew Michael Banta
Desk Top Publishers B-17 Banta @aol.com

War In The Air Stephan Coonts
Simon and Schuster New York

War To Be Won (A) Murray and Millett

Harvard Univ. Press Cambridge, Mass.

Doughty, John Lithographer
Full House-Aces High www.highironillustrations.com
This may be viewed and/or obtained, full-size
(38" x 26") in color, at the above address

Printed in Great Britain
by Amazon